Cligès

Cligès

Chrétien de Troyes

Translated from the Old French by
Burton Raffel

Afterword by Joseph J. Duggan

Yale University Press
New Haven & London

Set in Simoncini Garamond type by Tseng Information Systems, Inc., Durham, North Carolina. Printed in the United States of America by BookCrafters, Inc., Chelsea, Michigan.

Library of Congress Cataloging-in-Publication Data
Chrétien, de Troyes, 12th cent.
[Cligès. English]
Cligès / Chrétien de Troyes ; translated from the Old French by Burton Raffel ; afterword by Joseph J. Duggan.
p.   cm.
Includes bibliographical references.
ISBN 0-300-07020-9 (cloth : alk. paper). — ISBN 0-300-07021-7 (paper : alk. paper)
1. Romances—Translations into English.   2. Knights and knighthood—Romances.   3. Civilization, Medieval—Romances.   4. Arthurian romances.
I. Raffel, Burton.   II. Title.
PQ1445.C5E5   1997
841'.1—DC21   96-52694

A catalogue record for this book is available from the British Library.

The paper in this book meets the guidelines for permanence and durability of the Committee on Production Guidelines for Book Longevity of the Council on Library Resources.

10 9 8 7 6 5 4 3 2 1

For Brian, wherever he is

Contents

Translator's Preface

This is the third of Chrétien's great narratives I have trans-
lated. The first, *Yvain,* was published by Yale University Press in
1987; the second, *Erec and Enide,* was published, again by Yale,
in 1996. The publishers and I plan, over the next several years,
to produce versions of the two remaining poems.

Most of what needs to be explained about the technical
aspects of this translation has already been set out, in my Trans-
lator's Preface to *Yvain.* And as I also said there, "I will be con-
tent if this translation allows the modern reader some reason-
ably clear view of Chrétien's swift, clear style, his wonderfully
inventive story-telling, his perceptive characterizations and sure-
handed dialogue, his racy wit and sly irony, and the vividness
with which he evokes, for us his twentieth-century audiences,
the emotions and values of a flourishing, vibrant world." I need
only add that the longer I work with Chrétien, the more "mod-
ern" he seems to me, in virtually all his essential characteris-
tics—which may help to explain why, as I said in concluding
that prior Translator's Preface, "Chrétien is a delight to read—
and to translate." Not easy, but definitely a delight.

Although it is perhaps more usual to work from a single version of the text to be translated, I have chosen to translate from the two most recent editions of the Old French original, the *Oeuvres complètes* (1994), edited for Gallimard's deservedly famous Pléiade series by Daniel Poirion and five collaborating scholars, *Cligès* having been edited by Philippe Walter, and the complete *Romans* (1994), edited for Le Livre de Poche series, once again, by a team of scholars, *Cligès* being edited by Charles Méla and Olivier Collet. Although I have worked with both texts constantly open in front of me, picking and choosing what seemed to me, after years of translating Chrétien, to most accurately represent his style as I have come to know it, I have in general relied much more on the Poirion edition. I have consulted and (of course) shamelessly pillaged the helpful textual, historical, and literary notes in both editions.

Université des Acadiens
Lafayette, Louisiana

Cligès

Cil qui fist d'Érec et d'Énide,
Et les commandemanz d'Ovide
Et l'Art d'amors an romans mist,
Et le Mors de l'espaule fist,
Del roi Marc et d'Ysalt la blonde,
Et de la hupe et de l'aronde
Et del rossignol la muance,
Un novel conte rancommance

The poet who wrote of Erec
And Enide, and turned Ovid's
Remedies and his Art of Love
Into French, who wrote *The Shoulder*
Bite* and "The Tale of King Mark   5
And Iseult," and "The Transformation
Of the Swallow, the Nightingale,
And the Hoopoe Bird," now starts
Another tale of a young

*See "Pelops," in Ovid, *Metamorphoses,* book VI.

Greek knight, of Arthur's lineage.   10
But before we speak of him
I'll tell you his father's life,
Where he was from, and his bloodlines.
A man too noble and brave
To stay home, he left Greece   15
In search of fame and renown,
And went to England, then called
Britain. And the story I intend
To tell you I found on the shelves
Of the Holy Church of Saint Peter   20
At Beauvais, written in a book:
Chrétien of Troyes has drawn
His tale from those pages. And because
Those books are wonderfully old,
We know they're truthful; besides,   25
It's better to believe than not to.
Ancient books tell us all
We know of ancient history
And what life was like, back then.
And we've learned from those books that in Greece   30
Knighthood and learning ranked
Above all other things.
Ancient learning, like knighthood,
Passed from Greece to Rome,
And has reappeared, now,   35
In France. God give us the gift
To keep learning alive in a land
He smiles on, so France will never
Give up the honor she's won.
Others have gotten from God   40
What was only lent: no one

Speaks of Greeks or Romans,
Now: once their lives
Were snuffed out, so were their voices.

And here Chrétien begins   45
His story, as the book tells it:
It concerns a rich and honored
Emperor, the powerful ruler
Of both Greece and Constantinople.
His wise and noble empress   50
Had given him a pair of sons.
But the first was fully grown
When the second was born; he could
Have become a knight, had he wished,
And ruled the entire empire.   55
The name of the oldest son
Was Alexander; the younger
Was called Alis. And the father's
Name was Alexander;
The mother was Tantalis.   60
I've nothing much to say
Of Empress Tantalis,
Or her husband, or her younger son.
It's Alexander I'll deal with,
A man so brave and bold   65
He had no interest in becoming
A knight in his own country.
He'd heard stories of King
Arthur, then on the throne,
And the many noble barons   70
Who because it was famous all
Across the world, stayed

At his court. No matter how
He got there, or what he might
Endure in the process, no one   75
Could keep him from going. Of course,
Before he could journey to far-off
Britain and Cornwall, he needed
To say farewell to his father.
   So brave and bold Alexander   80
Went to speak to the emperor,
Seeking permission. He planned
To explain what he hoped to learn,
What he meant to do, in Britain.
"My father," he said, "in order   85
To better understand honor,
And win myself fame and renown,
I've come seeking a gift,
Which I beg you to grant me. And if
You consent, please say so now,   90
Without delay!" The emperor
Could see no harm in agreeing:
Indeed, nothing could be closer
To his heart than his son's honor.
It could only be right, he believed,   95
To give his consent. *Believed?*
Who could doubt it? What
Could be better than bringing honor
To his son? "I consent, my son.
Now tell me what you want me   100
To give you." And seeing that his passionate
Request had been granted, the gift
He'd longed for, and needed, would be his,
The emperor's son was delighted:

He'd have what he wanted. "My lord," 105
He said, "would you like to know
What your pledge means? First,
I'll need a lot of your gold
And silver, and many of your younger
Companions, men I should like 110
To choose myself, because,
Father, I plan to leave
Your empire and present myself
To the king who governs Britain,
And ask him to make me a knight. 115
I swear to you, Father, I'll never
Wear a visor over
My face, or a helmet on my head—
Never, until King Arthur
Buckles on my sword, 120
If he so chooses. No one
Else will make me a knight."
"Dear son, don't say such things!
This whole country is yours,
And rich Constantinople. 125
How can you think me a miser,
Giving you such a gift?
I'll have you crowned tomorrow,
And tomorrow you'll be a knight.
The whole of Greece will lie 130
In your hand, and all our barons,
As in duty they must, will vow
To serve and obey you. No sensible
Man could refuse such an offer."
    The young man listened. His father 135
Had promised to make him a knight

After Mass tomorrow. But he said
He'd rather prove himself
Brave or a coward in some country
Other than his own. "If you wish   140
To give me the gift I asked for,
Let me have furs and silks,
And good horses—because,
Before I can be a knight
I wish to serve King Arthur.   145
I'm not yet worthy of bearing
Arms. No one can dissuade me,
Whether by wheedling or flattery,
From traveling to that foreign land
And seeing for myself that king   150
And his barons, all so famous
For courtliness and courage.
Too many men of exalted
Station abandon, for sheer
Laziness, the fame they could   155
Have won, had they ventured out
In the world. Peace and fame
Are enemies, it seems to me,
For no man wins renown
Who spends his days quietly   160
At home. Weak men can't
Be brave; brave men won't
Be weak. They're opposite ways.
The man who sits and piles up
Wealth is a slave to his gold.   165
My father, whatever glory
I'm allowed to win is the only

Goal I can ever strive toward."
    The emperor was sad and delighted
At once, hearing these things— 170
Glad because his son
Had chosen the paths of courage,
But grieving because his son
Would soon be leaving him. But he'd made
A promise, and no matter how much 175
It hurt him to honor it, he had
No choice but to give his son
What he asked, for emperors can't lie.
"My son," he said, "how
Can I help my pleasure, seeing you 180
Drawn to honor and fame?
You may have, from my treasury, a pair
Of boats loaded with gold
And silver: always be open-
Handed, nobly generous, 185
And always be pleasant." His son
Rejoiced at the treasures he would have,
And understood his father's
Counsel of generous behavior
And liberal expenditure; 190
Then his father explained, "My son,
These are the things I believe:
Generosity's the queen
Of virtues, shedding its light
On all the others. That's easily 195
Proved. When will a rich man,
A wise man, escape reproach,
If he fails to share his wealth?

And who, having no wealth
But open hands, will fail   200
To be praised? The generous always
Win fame, but not the merely
High-born, polite, learned,
Noble, rich, strong,
Skilled at wielding weapons,   205
Powerful, brave, beautiful,
Or anything else, for just
As the fresh, newly blooming
Rose is the loveliest of flowers,
So, too, is generosity,   210
Surpassing every other
Virtue and shedding infinite
Grace on the good man,
Making him many times better.
But I can't tell you half   215
Of what needs to be said on this subject."
The young man had gotten all
He'd asked for and wanted, once
His father knew that his son
Was exactly what he wished him to be.   220
But the empress, his mother, was saddened,
Hearing the news that her son
Would soon be gone. Yet no one's
Sadness and sorrow could stop him,
Nor anyone's saying he was silly   225
And childish, nor any argument:
The young man ordered his boats
Made ready as soon as possible,
Not wanting to remain in his country
Any longer than he had to.   230

And as he'd ordered, that very
Night the boats were loaded
With meat and wine and biscuit.
      His boats were ready, and in
The morning, immensely happy,   235
Alexander and all
His companions came to the shore,
Everyone glad to be going.
Their escort was the emperor himself,
Along with the sorrowing empress.   240
The boats were moored below
A cliff; the sailors were waiting.
The sea was calm, with a gentle
Breeze, and the air was sweet.
As soon as he'd said farewell   245
To his father, and his mother, who was sick
To her very soul, the young man
Led his companions, in groups
Of four and three and two,
Across the sandy beach   250
And onto the boat, all of them
Eager to be on their way.
The sail was soon unfurled
And the anchor raised. And those
Left standing on shore, not happy   255
The young man was sailing away,
Followed the boats with their eyes
As best they could, and then,
Wanting to keep him in sight
As long as possible, climbed,   260
All of them together,
To a high hill close

To the sea, watching the cause
Of their sadness, their beloved son
And friend, until they could see   265
Nothing, praying that God
Would bring him to the port he wanted
And keep him safe from all danger.
          They sailed across the sea
All of April and part   270
Of May, arriving at Southampton
Almost without incident,
And late one morning dropped
Anchor in that port. Not
Accustomed to the weary life   275
Of waterborne travelers, and having
Been so long at sea,
All the young men reached shore
Sunburned, feeling exhausted
And weak, even the strongest   280
And healthiest among them. All
The same, they left the boats
Rejoicing both at escaping
The sea and arriving where they wanted
To be. But fatigued as they were,   285
They stayed in Southampton that night,
Immensely happy, and trying
To determine whether or not
King Arthur was then in England.
They were told they could find him at Winchester,   290
Not a very long journey
If they started early in the morning
And took the right road. They rose
Early the next morning and made themselves

Ready, equipment and all,   295
And then, as soon as they could,
They turned away from Southampton
And started down the straight
Road to Winchester, where they'd heard
King Arthur was staying. And even   300
Before it was nine o'clock,
The Greeks arrived at court.
Leaving their horses, and also
Their squires, in the courtyard below,
They climbed the stairs on foot,   305
Ascending toward the best
King the world has known
Or will ever know. And seeing
Them come, King Arthur was deeply
Pleased. But before presenting   310
Themselves, they unfastened their cloaks
And took them off, so no one
Would think they were fools. And only
Then were they willing to come
Before the king. The barons   315
At court all stared, obviously
Pleased by what they saw —
A group of handsome, noble
Youths, clearly all
The sons of counts and kings   320
(Which was, indeed, the truth),
Fine-featured, young, and tall,
Strong and well-made. Their clothes
Were cut to the same mold
And sewn from the same fabric,   325
Even the same color.

They were twelve in number, not counting
Their lord, of whom I will say
Only that no better man
Was ever born, neither proud   330
Nor pretentious. He stood in front
Of the king, wearing no cloak,
Then sank to his knees, and all
The others, honoring Arthur,
Went to their knees beside him.   335
     And Alexander, whose tongue
Was agile, and whose words were wise,
Greeted the king. "My lord,"
He said, "if your reputation
Is truly deserved, and your fame,   340
No king of such power, and with faith
In God, has been born on earth
Since the very first man was made.
My lord, your immense renown
Has brought me to your court to serve   345
And honor you, and here I wish
To remain, if my service pleases
You, until I've been made
A veritable knight—and only
By your own hand, and no other.   350
For if any one else makes me
A knight, I won't be a knight
In truth. O noble king,
If these pledges of service can lead you
To make me a knight, accept them,   355
Here and now, along with
The noble men I bring with me."
The king replied at once:

"My friend," he said, "I refuse
Neither you nor your men, 360
But cordially welcome you all.
You seem, and I think you are,
The sons of men of high rank.
Where are you from?" "From Greece."
"From Greece?" "Indeed." "And your father?" 365
"In truth, my lord, the emperor."
"Tell me your name, good friend."
"At the baptismal font, sprinkled
With salt, I was made a Christian
And given the name Alexander." 370
"Alexander, good friend,
I'm exceedingly happy to accept you
Into my service; you've done me
A very great honor, coming
To my court. I long to honor 375
You all as good men of standing.
You've been on your knees too long:
Rise, I command you! And from
This moment you all belong
To the inner circle of my court: 380
You've sailed to a welcoming port."
        The Greeks rose from the ground,
Delighted to receive so warm
A welcome from such a king.
And Alexander was fortunate, 385
His every desire fulfilled;
Arthur's barons warmly
Welcomed him, one and all.
And he, in turn, neither felt
Nor acted better than anyone 390

Else, greeting my lord
Gawain, then the others, in turn.
He endeared himself to them all,
Gawain even going
So far as to call him his friend.   395
The Greeks found excellent lodgings,
The best available, all
Together in a merchant's house.
Alexander had brought
With him enormous wealth,   400
And he kept constantly in mind
His father's wise advice,
His heart open to giving
Freely and spending well,
Duties he took most seriously.   405
Indeed, he worked at them hard
And long, living handsomely,
Giving much and spending
More, as his wealth required
And his heart urged him. The entire   410
Court was amazed, wondering
Where all this money came from.
He gave them expensive horses,
Carried from Greece. Devoting
Himself so intently to this cause,   415
And performing so well at court,
He won himself the king's
Friendship and respect, and the queen's,
And the barons'.
            Then Arthur decided
It was time to travel to Brittany.   420
He called his barons together,

Seeking their counsel, and asking
To whom he could trust the peace
And defense of England, until
He returned. As I understand it,   425
They gave a unanimous vote
For Count Angrès of Windsor
To command them, still convinced
That nowhere in all of England
Could anyone find a lord   430
More faithful, more loyal, more true.
So the count took care of the kingdom,
And Arthur and his queen, and her ladies,
Left, early the very
Next morning. Hearing the king   435
Would be coming, along with his barons,
All of Brittany rejoiced.
          The king's boat, as he made
The crossing, carried a single
Young man, Alexander, and only   440
A single girl, the queen's
Companion, Sordamour, who had always
Laughed at love. No one
Had ever heard her speak
Of a man worth loving, whether   445
For beauty, bravery, courage,
Rank, or any ability.
The girl was so gracious and lovely
That, if only she'd wanted them, she certainly
Should have been taking lessons   450
From Love. But it wasn't a subject
She wanted to study. This state
Of affairs saddened Love,

Which began to seriously consider
Revenge for the overweening   455
Pride she stubbornly displayed.
Love's aim was perfect: its arrow
Struck her right in the heart.
Her face changed color, her breath
Caught, and, despite herself,   460
She loved. She could not keep
Her eyes from Alexander,
Though she knew she had to be careful
Of my lord Gawain, her brother.
How dearly she paid and did penance   465
For her pride and disdain! Love drew her
A bath so burning hot
That her heart sweated and boiled.
Alexander was fine; Alexander
Was bad; she loved him, she didn't;   470
She accused her eyes of treason,
Saying, "Sight, you've betrayed me,
Escorting enemy invaders
To my heart. You used to be loyal,
But now what I see hurts me.   475
Hurts me? No, it helps me—
But if something hurts me, and I go
On looking, who controls my eyes?
Not me, I've lost the strength—
And how little I'm worth, unable   480
To tell my eyes where to look,
And when—for they look all the time.
I could save myself from Love,
Which wants to rule me: the heart
Can't hurt when the eyes can't see.   485

If I couldn't see him, he'd be gone.
But he's not. Yet he doesn't care:
If he did, he'd speak to me. He's never
Said he loves me: why love
Without being loved in return?   490
If his beauty captures my eyes,
And my eyes surrender, and stare,
Why should that mean I'm in love?
It's only a nightmare, a will-o-
The-wisp. My heart is free: 495
Nothing has happened. How
Could I love, simply with my eyes?
Yet how could my eyes wrong me,
Seeing what I want them to see?
Is that a sin? a crime? Never!   500
Can I scold my eyes for seeing?
The fault is mine: it's I
Who rule them. My eyes see nothing
Except what my heart tells them
To see. But my heart shouldn't want   505
Something that makes me suffer.
My heart makes my heart hurt.
Hurt? By God, I'm a fool,
Wanting what tears me apart.
Shouldn't I discard desire   510
That brings me pain? If I can.
If I can? What are you saying,
You fool? I'm not capable
Of much, if I can't control
Myself! Is Love, who's driven   515
So many insane, guiding
My steps? Let him lead others;

I've never been his, I never
Will be. He's nothing to me,
I've never wanted his friendship!"   520
     And so she tormented herself,
Loving and detesting, always
Doubting, unable to decide
Which road to take. She was sure
She knew how to fight off Love,   525
But no defenses worked.
Lord, if only she'd tried
Thinking Alexander's thoughts!
Love had given them each
An equal share of its gifts: 530
They'd been treated fairly and well,
Each of them loving the other.
If desire and longing had worked
As one, and together, love
Could have been faithful and true.   535
But she did not know her love
Was returned, or how he suffered.
     Observing them both, the queen
Often saw their color
Change, and their faces go pale,   540
But had no idea what was happening,
Unable to think of any
Reason other than the effect
Of travel at sea. She'd surely
Have seen more clearly, but the sea   545
Deceived her seeing, and she couldn't
See as they were seeing,
For all she saw was the sea,
And all they could see was love.

The queen could have blamed blindness,   550
Or love, or the sea, for the sickness
She saw, but blamed the sea,
As they did, each and all
Unable to see. How often
A sinless, innocent party   555
Is blamed, instead of sinners!
Here was the queen accusing
The sea of their sickness, too blind
To see that the sea was guilty
Of nothing. Until the ship   560
Was safely in port, Sordamour
Suffered in silence.
                As soon
As they landed, King Arthur knew
The people of Brittany rejoiced
At his coming, welcoming their rightful   565
Ruler and ready to serve him.
But I won't go on at any
Length about Arthur: instead,
You'll hear more of the two
Lovers tortured by Love,   570
Who'd engaged them both in battle.
      How Alexander longed
For the girl, who sighed for him!
But he knew nothing, and would
Not know until he'd suffered   575
And groaned a good deal longer.
His love led him to serve
The queen and all her young ladies,
But never allowed him to speak
To the one who filled his thoughts.   580

And if she had dared tell him
How she longed to claim him for her own,
He'd gladly have spilled out his heart,
But she couldn't, and didn't, speak.
Constantly seeing each other,   585
Yet unable to speak or act,
Kept pulling them this way and that,
Feeding and inflaming their love.
But all lovers are forever
Feeding love with their eyes,   590
When they can't do more than look,
And they feel, in the pleasure this gives them,
Flaring the flames higher,
That love becomes better. But it's worse:
Whoever comes closer and closer   595
To a fire is easier for the flames
To reach than he who holds back.
And so their love kept growing,
Although they hid it, afraid
To reveal what they felt, neither   600
Seeing the flame and smoke
Burning under the ashes.
Fire loses no heat,
Covered with cinders, but lasts
Longer and glows hotter.   605
How they suffered! And yet,
Determined to tell no one,
Have no one aware of their longing,
They spent their days deceiving
Everyone, concealing their pain.   610
But at night suffering overflowed
Their hearts and filled their minds.

Let me tell you, first, the unspoken
Words he said to himself
As Love conjured pictures   615
Of her for whom he was suffering,
So wounding his heart that even
Lying in bed he could not
Sleep, yet happily remembering
That face, that beauty he never   620
Expected could ever be his:
"I ought to consider myself
A fool," he said to himself.
"A fool? And why not? I'm afraid
To say what my heart feels,   625
For fear speaking would make it
Worse. And yet concealment
And silence are better, for speech
Would reveal me as the fool I am.
Will no one ever know?   630
If I keep it forever hidden —
If no one knows my pain —
How will I find relief?
The height of folly is a sick man
Reluctant to hunt for health,   635
Though he knows where to find it. The fool
Thinks he can cure himself
And get what he wants by running
After what hurt him. But why
Go seeking help if you don't   640
Believe there's a cure? Why thrash
Around for nothing? This wound
Feels so deep, so wide,
That nothing will ever cure it —

No potion, no ointment, no medicine   645
Made of leaves or roots.
There are wounds that never heal,
And this one goes so deep
That nothing can help it. Nothing?
Perhaps I'm lying to myself.   650
The moment I felt this sickness
I might have found a willing
Physician, had I dared to show
What I felt, had I dared to speak.
But the case would be hard to argue: 655
She might have refused to listen
And scorned the fee I could pay.
It's hardly surprising if I'm troubled:
I'm hurt to the heart and ruled
By my sickness, not knowing its name.   660
Where do these pains come from?
But surely I know just where:
It's Love Himself who's done this.
Love? Love is hurtful?
Isn't he gracious and sweet?   665
I'd thought that what one found
In love was kind and good,
But Love's been proven a traitor.
No one who doesn't know
Its ways would believe its tricks.   670
All its recruits are fools,
For Love constantly wounds
Its faithful. It knows nothing of honor.
It plays dangerous games,
Painful, sorrowful amusement.   675
Now what do I do? Retreat?

It might be the safest move,
But how on earth is it managed?
If Love is threatening, punishing,
In order to teach me, shape me,   680
Can I turn my back on my teacher?
That would be folly indeed!
Whatever it wants to teach me
I need to work at my lessons:
Think how much I could learn.   685
But it hurts so much, and that's bad.
'But where are the wounds?' I see none.
'Then why complain? Isn't that
Wrong?' No: Your arrows
Pierced me deep in the heart,   690
And you won't pull them out. 'How
Can an arrow have pierced your body
And left no mark on your skin?
Answer me that, go on!
Where are you wounded?' In the eye.   695
'In the eye? And you're still alive?'
It's not the eye that was hurt,
But the heart: that's where it went.
'Now tell me, please, just how
The arrow got to your heart   700
Without destroying your eye?
Could the arrow pass through your eye
And the heart in your belly hurt
While the eye, which felt the first blow,
Feels no pain?' That's easily   705
Explained: eyes don't have
To worry, they do nothing
By themselves, and yet the eye

Is the heart's mirror, so the arrow
Reaches the heart through its mirror,   710
Doing no damage to the eye,
Yet the feeling hurts the heart.
The heart sits in the body
Like a candle set inside
A lantern. Blow out the candle   715
And there's no more light in the lantern.
But just as long as the candle
Burns, the lantern keeps off
The dark, and the flame lighting it
Up from inside neither   720
Harms nor destroys it. Glass
Is exactly the same: no matter
How strong it may be, the sun's
Rays can always pierce it,
Without the glass being damaged.   725
And yet the glass is never
So clear that, without being pierced,
It can shed any light. The eyes
Are much like the glass and the lantern:
The world's glow strikes   730
Against them just at the spot
Where the heart is watching, and it sees
What's out there, whatever it is.
It sees all sorts of things,
Some of them green, some violet,   735
Some red, and others blue;
It likes some, which are sweet,
And dislikes others, which are ugly.
But whatever shines in the mirror
And pleases it most can also   740

Betray it, unless it's careful.
My eyes have been deceived,
For what my heart saw
In their mirror was a light that brought me
Darkness, and now it's inside me,   745
And it's making my heart fail me.
My once-friendly heart has led me
Astray, gone over to the enemy.
I can call it a criminal, for to me,
Indeed, it's been spiteful and cruel.   750
I thought I had three friends,
One heart, two eyes, all working
Together, but now I think
They hate me. Oh God, who
Are my friends, if these are my foes?   755
They're mine, yet they're trying to kill me.
These servants of mine are over-
Confident, pleasing themselves
Instead of me. Seeing
How they leave me uncared for, I know   760
How true it is that a good
Master loses his love
When bad servants mistreat him.
Sooner or later, whoever
Deals with a bad servant   765
Finds himself complaining.
          "But back to that arrow, especially
Fashioned for me, and in me
Now: what is it like?
I'm not sure I can truly   770
Say, for the work was wonderfully
Done: it's hardly surprising

I doubt my own words, though I'll try
Hard to tell you what I know.
The notch at the end of the shaft   775
And the feathers are so close, if you look
Carefully, that the space between
Is barely a knife blade thick,
So straight and even that it's easy
To see how perfectly crafted   780
And without mistake it was made.
The feathers seem so vividly
Colored they look like gold,
But no one needed to gild them,
Please believe me, for they gleam   785
By themselves, brighter than gold:
They're three blond hairs that I saw,
Not long ago, at sea.
And this is the bitter arrow
Of love. God, how rich   790
And precious! Who, having
Such wealth, for the rest of his life
Could want for any other
Riches? Myself, I can swear
There's nothing more to desire: 795
Having these feathers, I wouldn't
Trade them for the whole city
Of Antioch. And if these are worth
So much, how can one put
A price on all the rest?   800
So utterly beautiful, charming,
So good, so perfect, so dear
That, even now, I long
To see myself reflected

In the mirror of that face God   805
Has made so clear that no glass,
No emerald, no topaz, can equal it.
But even that can't match
The light shining from her eyes,
Which seem to anyone who sees them   810
Like a pair of glowing candles.
And where is the tongue so eloquent
It can tell, as they should be told,
Of her limpid complexion, her lovely
Nose? For just as the rose   815
Outshines the lily, her face
Turns the lily dark. And her laughing
Little mouth, fashioned
By God so no one can see her
Without knowing that her heart   820
Is alive with laughter? How
Describe the teeth in that mouth?
Set so smoothly together
They seem like one, not many—
And to make them more dazzling, Nature   825
Crafted another work
Of art: seeing those lips
Open, you'd have to say
Her teeth were ivory, or silver.
But so much needs to be said   830
To show you each and every
Part—her chin—her ears—
That who could be surprised
To find me forgetting something?
Should I bother telling you how crystal   835
Seems dark and murky, next

To her throat? That under her hair
Her neck is eight times whiter
Than ivory? Then, from the base
Of her throat to the top of her bodice,   840
I see a bit of uncovered
Breast, whiter than snow.
There'd be no sorrow left,
Had I seen all of Love's barb:
I could tell you, then, exactly   845
How it was made, and of what.
But I haven't, so it's not my fault
That I can't fully describe
What I've never fully seen.
Love has only shown me   850
Feathers, and the notch in the shaft,
For the arrow was left in its quiver—
That is, in the clothes the girl
Was wearing. And there, by God,
Is the sickness that's killing me, the pointed   855
Stick, the radiant beam,
Driven so wickedly deep
In my heart. What right can I have
To resent it? My link with Love
Is tied too tight for quarreling,   860
For fighting. It will last forever.
He'll do with me just as he wishes,
As he always does, and must,
And as I wish he would,
For I have no hunger to be cured.   865
And I'd rather never be healthy
Again, but remain in his power,
Than be healed at the hands of anyone

But she who first infected me."
    And thus Alexander indicted   870
Love at great length. But Sordamour's
Complaint was just as long.
She tossed and turned all night,
Unable to sleep or rest.
Love was locked in her heart,   875
Causing a raging battle
That shook the depth of her being
And brought her such pain and distress
That she wept from dusk to dawn,
So racked and wrung that her heart   880
Almost stopped beating. And after
All that struggling and torment,
Those floods of tears and wrenching
Sighs and yawns, when she looked
Deep in her heart what she saw   885
Was the image of him for whom
She was tortured. A moment of relief,
Of comfort, a very few happy
Thoughts, and then, as she lay there
Quietly, her mood shifted   890
And her mind turned those pleasant
Fancies back into folly,
And she began to complain once more,
Saying: "Fool! What difference
Does it make that he's so noble,   895
So generous, courteous, and brave?
He does himself honor. Of course!
What good does his beauty do *me?*
It's his affair, that's all!
It has no connection with me,   900

It gives me nothing. Nothing?
No, and that's what I want!
If he were as wise as Solomon,
And Nature had showered on his head
Every kind of beauty   905
A man can possess, and then God
Blessed me with the power, if I chose,
To destroy it all with a word,
I wouldn't, not to him—
No, I'd be glad, if I could,   910
To make him better still.
Lord! I really don't hate him.
It doesn't mean I love him.
No! Not him, or anyone!
But why do I think of him,   915
If he isn't particularly pleasing?
I don't know, I'm all confused,
For I've never thought so much
About any man alive,
And I long to see him every   920
Day, and I'm always staring,
And how I like what I see!
Could that be Love? Yes,
It could—for why would I always
Be thinking of him and no one   925
Else? I'm in love, I am!
And he's the one I'd want
To love, if he wants to be loved.
What a wicked thought—but Love
Has so overwhelmed me I've become   930
A fool, and my mind won't work;
I've no defenses left,

I'm obliged to yield. I've tried
So hard and so long to harden
Myself against him, as I should,   935
That I've never let myself think
Like a lover. But now I want to.
What kind of affection could he feel
If, in loving me, he received
No favor, no attentions, in return?   940
My pride's been tamed by his powers;
I'm obliged to do as he wishes.
So I want to love him, I want him
To rule me, I'm learning Love.
But how? What should I do   945
For him? Oh, but I know,
I'm already learned and wise
In such things, no one need teach me;
There's nothing more to be taught.
It was Love's plan, and my   950
Desire, that because I love
This man, I should lose my pride
And be wise and charming and gracious
To everyone. Can one man make me
Be loving to all? Gracious   955
To all, yes, but Love's
Lessons don't teach me to love
Everyone. I'm taught to do good things,
Not bad. I wasn't named
Sordamour* by accident!   960
I must love, and I must be loved,
And my name proves it, for 'love'

Amour = "love"; *de* (here elided to *d'*) = "of."

Is part of my name. Nor is it
Accidental that the first
Part of my name bears   965
The meaning 'gold,' ** for the best
Gold shines the brightest.
My name is all the better
For not containing some color
That clashes with gold, but belongs   970
To the purest in both gold and Love:
Whenever 'Sordamour'
Is spoken, love is reborn,
One part of my name gilding
The other with shining gold,   975
So in saying 'Sordamour'
You say 'covered over with love.'
But the dazzling gleam of gold
Can't be as bright as the light
Of this love by which Love has honored   980
Me, making me gold
With his glow: I'll strive to honor
That gift, so Love need never
Complain of me. I'm in love
Now; I'll be in love forever.   985
With whom? Ah, a fine
Question! With the one Love tells me
To love, and no one else.
But what's the use, if he never
Knows unless I tell him?   990
And what should I do: beg him?
Whoever truly desires

**Sor* = "bright or golden blonde."

Something is supposed to ask for it.
What? Shall I ask him to love me?
Never. And why? No woman   995
Makes the mistake of asking
A man for his love, unless
She's totally out of her mind.
The world would know I was mad,
If I ever permitted my mouth   1000
To speak such scandalous words.
And if he heard me speak
My love, he'd think me vile,
He'd never let me forget
That I was the one to speak first.   1005
How could I let my love
Be so vile that I begged him to love me?
He'll love me more, in the end.
Yet Lord! How will he ever
Know if I never tell him?   1010
But I haven't suffered enough
To trouble my mind with such thoughts.
I need to wait until,
Somehow, he knows. I'll never
Tell him. Surely he'll see,   1015
If he's ever been in love,
Or heard what love is like.
Heard? I'm talking nonsense.
Love is never generous
Enough to make us wise   1020
By words, but only by experience.
That's something I understand:
No one studies this subject
Like a lesson, or profits from gossip

And words. The lessons I could have been   1025
Learning, going to school
With love! But I stayed away,
So love's now teaching me love—
But who teaches an ox how to plow!
The thing that worries me most   1030
Is perhaps my lover has never
Loved or been loved, and if so,
I'm sowing seed in the ocean,
Where seeds don't grow. But there's nothing
More to be done; I must wait   1035
And suffer until I see
If looks and subtle words
Can make him understand.
I'll do what I can to let him
See he can have my love   1040
If he asks, if he dares. That's all
I can do: love him and be his.
He may not love me. But I'll
Love him."
            And so they complained,
And hid their love from each other.   1045
Their days were bad, their nights
Worse. And so they stayed
In Brittany, and stayed sorrowful,
A long time, till summer
Ended. Early in October   1050
A messenger came from London
And Canterbury, through Dover, bringing
The king troublesome news.
He told Arthur he needed
To be back in Britain, for the governor   1055

He'd left in command was trying
To take away his throne;
He'd already gathered a great
Army, from his lands and his friends,
And brought them all to London   1060
To keep the king, if he could,
From ever coming back.
              Hearing this news, the king,
Wild with anger, immediately
Summoned his barons to council.   1065
And to heighten their resolve,
And make them anxious to defeat
The traitor, he told them this trouble
And fighting was entirely their fault,
For their advice had been   1070
To entrust his kingdom to this criminal
Who was even worse than Ganelon.*
None of the barons denied
The accusation, for indeed
They'd given exactly that counsel.   1075
But now, they assured the king,
Angrès would be forced into exile;
No town or fortified castle
Could keep him safe, for they'd drive
Him out. One and all   1080
They declared to the king, and swore
In solemn oaths, they'd capture
The traitor or never again
Hold land that the king had granted.
And the king had it proclaimed   1085

*Who, in *La Chanson de Roland,* betrays Roland.

All across the country
That no one who could carry arms
Should stay at home, but join Arthur
And his army in England. All
Of Brittany was excited; no army   1090
Of such a size had ever
Been seen. As the boats set sail
It seemed, from the tumult and shouting,
That every man in Brittany
Had come on board: the very   1095
Waves of the sea became
Invisible, covered with so many
Ships. War was certain.
      The Channel crossed, the hordes
Of Arthur's army prepared   1100
To camp on the shore. It occurred
To Alexander to go
To the king and beg to be knighted,
For if fame with all its rewards
Was ever to be won, here   1105
And now in England was when
He could win it. He took his Greek
Companions with him, all of them
Anxious to have it done.
They found the king at his tent—   1110
In fact, standing in front of it.
And when he saw the Greeks
Approach, he called them to him:
"Gentlemen," he said, "don't hide
Your intentions. What do you need?"   1115
Speaking for himself as well as
The others, Alexander replied,

"Your Majesty, I've come to ask,
If you as our lord and master
Wish it, to dub us knights,   1120
Myself and all my companions."
"Willingly, very willingly,"
Said the king. "And since you've asked me,
Let's waste no time!" Arthur
Ordered equipment for thirteen   1125
Knights to be brought at once.
The king's commands were obeyed,
And as each of them asked for whatever
He needed—arms and armor
And horses—Arthur gave each,   1130
As a gift, all that was wanted.
And all were grateful to accept them.
Nor were these casual gifts,
But worth enormous sums.
Yet anyone buying or selling   1135
The equipment given to the young
Leader of the Greeks would have found
It was worth as much as the others
Combined. Then they took off their clothes
And there on the shore washed   1140
And bathed, for they'd let no one
Heat them water: the sea,
They said, would be bath and bathwater.
The queen, whose feelings for the young
Greek were hardly hostile,   1145
For she loved him dearly, was told,
And wanting to make him a handsome
Present (finer in the event
Than she knew) emptied her treasure

Chests and found him a white 1150
Silk shirt, beautifully sewn,
Delicate and wonderfully soft.
Every inch of embroidery
Was either gold or silver.
Sordamour had helped 1155
With the sewing, from time to time:
In both sleeves, and the collar,
She'd set a strand of her hair
Beside the golden thread,
Wanting to see if a man, 1160
Looking particularly closely,
Could see they weren't the same,
For though they were much alike
A careful eye could see
That her hair shone brighter. The queen 1165
Ordered the shirt brought
To Alexander. But Lord!
How happy the Greek would have been,
Had he known what the queen was giving him!
And she who'd sewn the shirt, 1170
If only she'd known her beloved
Would have it, and wear it, would have known
Joy just as great.
It would have brought her the deepest
Comfort; she couldn't have loved 1175
All the rest of her hair
As much as the strands he wore.
But neither one of them knew
A thing about it: what
A painful ignorance! The queen's 1180
Messenger carried the shirt

To the shore, where the young men were bathing,
And finding Alexander in the water,
Offered him the shirt,
Which the young man gladly accepted,   1185
For a gift from the queen herself
Was doubly dear and welcome.
But had he known the rest
He'd have thought it worth much more;
He wouldn't have exchanged it, I think,   1190
With any man alive;
He'd have made it a holy shrine
Where he worshiped day and night.
Without the slightest delay
He put it on. And when   1195
He was dressed and ready, he
And all his Greek companions
Returned to the king's tent.
The queen (if I have it right)
Was sitting there, wanting   1200
To watch the brand-new knights
Arriving. All were handsome
Young men, but without any question
Alexander, with his perfect
Body, possessed more beauty   1205
Than any.
          They became knights:
What more can I say? Let me turn
To the king and the army that came
To London. Most of his people
Were loyal, and flocked to his side.   1210
Count Angrès assembled his forces—
At least, those he could keep

With gifts and promises. And knowing
Some of his men didn't love him,
And some would prove disloyal,   1215
Under cover of darkness he fled.
But before they abandoned London
He ransacked the city for all
The food and silver and gold
He could get, and shared it out   1220
With his men. News of his flight
Was brought to the king: Angrès
And his men were gone, taking
With them as much of the city's
Food and all the loot   1225
They could carry, leaving the merchants
And everyone else ruined,
With their larders bare and their purses
Empty. And the king declared
He'd take no ransom for Angrès   1230
But hang the traitor as soon
As he caught him, if only he could.
The army immediately marched
To Angrès's castle at Windsor.
Whatever it's like today,   1235
In those days it wasn't a castle
Easily captured, if defenders
Fought hard, and as soon as Angrès
Conceived his treason, he'd had it
Fortified with moats,   1240
And with double walls braced
Behind by strong stakes,
So catapulted stones
Couldn't smash them. He'd spared no cost.

June and July and August   1245
Had been spent in setting up
Drawbridges, making fences,
Digging trenches, and building
Barriers and sliding iron
Grates for the doors, and a stone   1250
Tower. The gates had never
Been shut, either in fear
Or to keep out an enemy. The castle
Stood on a height, with the River
Thames below it. Arthur's   1255
Army camped on the banks,
Put up their tents, and made ready.
The whole plain was covered
With brightly colored tents,
Red and green, glittering   1260
In the hot sun, reflected
Along the length of the river
For miles and miles. The castle
Defenders, to amuse themselves,
Came down to the shore, carrying   1265
Spears in their hands, with their shields
Pressed against their chests,
And no other weapons, wanting
To show, by this display,
How little they had to fear,   1270
Going about disarmed.
          Watching from the other shore,
As his enemies played at war
Right under his eyes, Alexander
Felt more like fighting than playing,   1275
So he called to the other Greeks,

One after another, by name —
Cornin, first, whom he dearly
Loved, then Acor the Fearless,
And Nabunal from Mycenae,   1280
And Acoridome from Athens,
And Ferlin from Salonika,
And Charquedon, who came from Africa,
And Parmenides, and Francal,
Torin the Strong, Pinagel,   1285
Nerice, and Neriolis:
"Gentlemen," he said, "I'd like
To introduce my sword
And spear to those fellows I see
Playing right over there.   1290
They don't appear to think
We're good for much, or they wouldn't
Amuse themselves as they're doing,
Almost unarmed. As brand-new
Knights we've had no chance   1295
To use our weapons on other
Knights or even on training
Posts. These fresh new lances
Have lain too long unused.
What were our shields made for?   1300
They've never been bent or broken.
But these are all worthless
Unless they're used in battle!
Let's cross the ford, and attack them."
They cried, "You can count on us!"   1305
Then said, "As God is our Savior,
Your friends don't desert you."
They buckled on their swords,

Saddled and bridled their horses,
Then mounted and took up their shields,   1310
Hung them around their necks,
Then raised their spears (all painted
The same color, as were
Their shields) and rushed as one
To the ford. Their enemies quickly   1315
Set their lances, ready
To fight, but the Greeks did well,
Not waiting, not holding back,
Nor giving up a foot
Of ground, but striking the defenders   1320
So fiercely that even their best
Fighters were driven from their saddles.
They'd taken the Greeks for boys,
Worthless dolts and cowards,
But their first assault wasn't wasted,   1325
For thirteen defenders fell.
Arthur's army began
To buzz with word of their bravery.
There might have been some fine
Fighting, had the enemy lingered,   1330
For warriors ran for their weapons
And excited sounds rose up,
But the enemy ran for their lives,
Thinking it safer to leave.
The Greeks followed after,   1335
Striking with swords and spears;
Many heads were severed,
But Alexander did best,
Leading away four
Captives, bound together.   1340

The dead lay where they'd fallen,
Many without their heads,
All of them cut and slashed.
        To celebrate, as he should,
His first victories, Alexander   1345
Brought his prisoners to the queen,
Not wanting the king to know
They'd been taken: Arthur would hang them.
The queen ordered them locked
Away as traitors. All   1350
Around the army they talked
Of the Greeks, commending the fine
Manners and courtesy shown
To his prisoners by Alexander,
Handing them over to the queen   1355
And not the king, who surely
Would have had them hanged on the spot.
But the king was not very happy.
He immediately sent for the queen
To discuss the matter and demand   1360
She release the traitors to him:
For her to hold them would be strongly
Against his wishes. The queen
Came at his call, and they talked,
As they had to, of what might be done   1365
With the traitors. The Greeks remained
Behind, in the queen's tent,
Along with her maidens, and all
Twelve of them chatted with the girls,
But Alexander said nothing.   1370
Seated near him, Sordamour
Noted his silence. Her cheek

Resting on her hand, she seemed
Lost in thought. And so
She sat for a while, until   1375
She saw, both at his arm
And his neck, the hair she'd used
As a thread, in sewing his shirt.
She came a little closer,
For now she had an excuse   1380
To begin a conversation.
But how to begin? She couldn't
Find the first words,
So she said to herself: "How
Can I start, what can I say?   1385
Should I use his name or call him
Beloved? Beloved? No!
Then how? I'll use his name.
Oh Lord, how sweet it would be
To call him Beloved! If only   1390
I dared make that claim.
Dared? Who can stop me?
I'm afraid it might be a lie.
A lie? Who knows if it is?
But if it is, I'll be sorry.   1395
I don't want to lie
And it's better just to admit it.
But God, *he* wouldn't be lying
If he called me his beloved!
And I, would I be lying?   1400
We both should tell the truth,
But the fault would be his, if I lied.
Yet why should his name be so hard
To say that I long to tell him

The truth? His name is too long,   1405
I'd find myself stuck in the middle.
All the same, if I called him
Beloved, I'd say his whole name.
Why should I tremble at his other
Name, but think it so easy   1410
To risk my life and call him
Beloved?" She lingered so long
On these thoughts that the queen came back
From her meeting with the king. Seeing her
Come, Alexander went   1415
To ask what the king had commanded
And what would now be done.
"My dear," she said, "he's ordered
Me to hand them over,
So justice and law can prevail.   1420
The king was angry with me,
Very angry, for not
Delivering the prisoners.
I have no choice but to give them
Up, since he wants them for himself."   1425
Which was what happened that day.
And the day after, the king
Called his good and loyal
Knights to the royal tent,
To pass lawful judgment   1430
On the four traitors, deciding
How they should suffer and die.
Some wanted them flayed
Alive, some wanted them hanged
Or burned; the king himself   1435
Preferred to have them drawn

And quartered. Then they sent for the prisoners,
And had them bound, and the king
Declared they'd be cut apart
In front of the castle, so the defenders   1440
Inside could see how they died.
Justice was thus decided,
As the king wanted it done.
Then Arthur withdrew to his living
Quarters, and summoned Alexander,   1445
Calling him his great good friend:
"Yesterday," he said, "I saw you
Attacking and defending wonderfully
Well. You deserve a reward.
I hereby add to the force   1450
You command half a thousand
Welsh knights and a thousand British
Soldiers. When I've ended my war,
In addition to all I've given you,
I plan to crown you ruler   1455
Of the best kingdom in Wales.
I'll give you castles and towns,
Cities and palaces, to hold
Until you return to the lands
Your father rules and where,   1460
By right, you'll be emperor."
Alexander warmly
Thanked the king, as did
The Greeks who served him. And all
Of Arthur's barons declared   1465
The young man richly deserved
Whatever honors the king
Had granted him. When Alexander

Saw the host of knights
And soldiers he now commanded,   1470
He ordered fanfares of horns
And trumpets throughout the camp.
Good men and bad, no one
Refused to take up arms:
Welshmen and Bretons, men   1475
Of Scotland and Cornwall, flocked
To his banner, for now his forces
Amounted to a potent army.
And now the Thames began
To go dry, for it had not rained   1480
All summer, England was parched,
Fish died, and boats
Sank into mud at their docks.
Whoever cared to could cross
The ford at any point.   1485
Arthur's army poured
Across; some seized the valley,
Some took the outer bulwarks;
And those who held the castle
Could only stare at the incredible   1490
Horde opposing them, well
Prepared to destroy their fortress.
They made their defenses ready.
But before he ordered the assault,
The king commanded each of the   1495
Traitors tied to four horses
And pulled to pieces, dragged
Through valleys and highlands and hills.
And Count Angrès grew angry,
Forced to watch men   1500

Dear to him torn apart.
The other defenders were frightened,
But even fear couldn't make them
Anxious to surrender: they were forced
To defend the castle as fiercely   1505
As they could, for the king had clearly
Shown them the depth of his anger,
And they saw, if he took them prisoner,
They'd die miserable deaths.
When the four traitors were lying   1510
In pieces, scattered all over,
The king's army attacked.
Nothing went well, at first:
They hurled all sorts of missiles
Into the castle—boulders   1515
And heavy spears, and they fired
Burning arrows, but accomplished
Little, hard as they tried.
Crossbows and slings sent clattering
Bolts and stones all over,   1520
Arrows and round pellets
Came flying out of the sky
Like rain mixed with hail.
And so they labored, all day,
One side attacking, the other   1525
Defending, until darkness stopped them.
And the king announced to the army,
Had it proclaimed across
The camp, what rewards were waiting:
"To whoever captures the castle   1530
I'll give a bejeweled cup
Worth fifteen ounces of gold,

The most precious I own — a beautiful,
Costly cup. And whoever
Wins it will take as much   1535
Delight in how it is made
As the rare and expensive materials:
The workmanship is magnificent.
But to tell the truth, the gems
Studded across it are worth   1540
More than its craft or its gold.
Whoever takes the castle
Will have it, even a simple
Soldier. And if it's a knight,
Whatever he asks for, above   1545
And beyond the cup, will be his,
As long as it's of this world."
          After hearing what the heralds said,
Alexander, who made it a habit
To visit the queen each night,   1550
Came to see her, as he always
Did. They sat together,
Side by side, the queen
And Alexander. And near them,
Seated all alone,   1555
Was Sordamour, so glad
To see him she wouldn't have changed
Her place for one in heaven.
Taking Alexander's
Hand, the queen glanced   1560
At the gold thread, which had worn
Badly. But as it dulled,
The golden hair gleamed
More brightly. Then, as it happened,

The queen recalled who'd sewn   1565
The garment, and began to laugh.
The Greek was startled, and begged her,
Please, if she could, to tell him
What struck her as so amusing.
Hesitating a moment,   1570
The queen looked at her maid,
Calling the girl closer.
Sordamour came at once,
Happy to kneel beside her.
And Alexander was thrilled,   1575
Seeing her come so close
That he could have touched her, but lacked
The courage required to look
Steadily in her direction.
His senses almost failed him;   1580
He breathed but could not speak.
And she, for her part, was stunned
And could not use her eyes,
Which stared straight at the ground,
Not even blinking. The queen   1585
Was truly startled, watching
The girl turn white, then red.
She looked with great care from one
To the other, studying their faces,
Observing their colors change.   1590
It seemed to her, without
Much question, these shifting hues
Were clearly the signs of love,
But wishing to make no trouble
She pretended to see nothing   1595
Of what she so plainly saw.

She did exactly as she should,
Her face showing not a thing,
And simply said to the girl,
"My dear, come look, and tell me   1600
The plain truth. Where
Was this shirt sewn, the one
This knight is wearing? And if you
Had a hand in its making, was something
Of your own added?" Although   1605
The girl burned with anguish
And shame, she was glad to tell
The story; she wanted him to hear
The truth—and hearing it made him
So happy, listening as she told   1610
How the shirt had been made, it was hard
To keep himself from falling
To his knees and worshiping those strands
Of her hair, now that he knew them.
The loyal Greeks who were with him,   1615
And the queen herself, seemed to him
Sources of pain and torment.
Their presence kept him from pressing
The precious fabric to his eyes
And his lips, as he hungered to do,   1620
But only if no one was watching.
Having this much of his loved one
Was enough, for he never expected
Anything more. Desire
Filled him with fear, but as soon   1625
As he could, free of his friends,
He kissed it a hundred thousand
Times, sure he'd been born

Under a lucky star.
And thus he was happy all night,   1630
Though careful to let no one see.
Lying in his bed, this thing
Which could give no delight delighted
Him, offered him solace
And joy. He held it all night,   1635
And every time he looked
It made him feel lord of the world.
When warriors find rapture in a hair,
Love has turned wise men to fools.
But he will find a new pleasure: 1640
This one will fade.
        Before
The clear dawn, and the bright hot sun,
The traitors took counsel together:
What could they, what should they do?
Surely, they could hold the castle   1645
For a long, long time, if they tried,
But knowing the king's proud heart
They knew he'd besiege them the rest
Of his life, until he had won,
And when he had won they'd be dead.   1650
They couldn't surrender: the king
Would show them no mercy. Whatever
Might happen, all their options
Were bad: whichever way
They looked there was nothing but death.   1655
And so they decided that the very
Next day, before it was light,
They would stage a secret attack,
Hoping Arthur's army

Were asleep and unarmed, his knights   1660
Lying asleep in their beds.
Caught before they awakened,
Neither equipped nor ready,
Arthur's host could be slaughtered
So savagely that no one would ever   1665
Forget this night of killing.
The traitors plotted this desperate
Assault, to which all agreed,
Convinced that their lives would be worthless
Without it. They were all resolved,   1670
No matter what, to fight
Fiercely, finding no other
Ending but death or imprisonment.
They knew it was not the safest
Path, not guaranteed   1675
To succeed, but what better way
Was there? Flight was impossible:
The enemy, as well as the water,
Had them surrounded, trapped
In the middle. The decision taken,   1680
There was no delay: they took up
Arms and left at once,
Through an ancient western gate
They hoped the army would least
Suspect and would not be watching.   1685
They took up battle positions,
Forming five battalions
Of at least two thousand soldiers
Each, all of them armed
To the teeth, and a thousand knights.   1690
The moon had not risen, that night,

And the stars shed no light,
But before they reached the tents
Up came the moon—because,
I believe, it was sent to hurt them,   1695
Rising earlier than usual,
So God, who meant to destroy them,
Could light up the darkness, for He had
No love for them or their cause,
But hated them all for their mortal   1700
Sins, for traitors and treason
Are especially loathsome in His eyes.
And so He commanded the moon
To shine, in order to destroy them.
And the moonlight brought them disaster,   1705
Glittering on their swords and shields
And gleaming even more brightly
On their helmets, for the sentinels, protecting
The army in the dark, saw them,
And began calling and shouting: 1710
"Up, up, knights! Awake!
Take up your weapons! The traitors
Are here, attacking!" And the whole
Army awoke and ran
For their weapons, hurrying, as they had to,   1715
In such a situation—
But no one rushed out alone,
Each waited for the rest to be ready.
The knights mounted their horses.
Meanwhile, the nighttime attackers   1720
Hurried, trying to make
Their assault good; to surprise,
Disarmed, whomever they could.

Their forces were divided in five
Groups, as I've said: one   1725
Near the edge of the wood,
One along the river,
The third coming across
The plain, the fourth in the valley,
And the fifth hurrying through   1730
A rocky gap, hoping
To strike at the tents unopposed.
But the road was not as easy
As they wanted, nor as safe,
For loyal troops intervened   1735
And fought them fiercely, angry
At the traitors, hurling insults.
They clashed violently, striking
Each other with their sharp lances,
Smashing, banging, throwing   1740
Themselves into battle as wildly
As lions hunting prey,
Or even wilder, gulping
Down whatever their claws
Can catch. This first assault   1745
Left many men of both
Armies lying dead,
But reinforcements reached
The traitors, who stood their ground
And sold their lives at good   1750
Prices. They were almost beaten,
But the other four battalions
Came to their rescue. The loyal
Knights charged them, riding
As fast as their horses would run;   1755

They rained so many blows
On the traitors' shields that, aside
From the wounded, more than five hundred
Fell. The Greeks spared
No one, and Alexander   1760
Kept his weapons busy.
At the height of the battle, he attacked
One of the rascals, a fellow
As worthless as a button, whose helmet
And shield helped him as much   1765
As Persian silk. Having done
His business, the Greek offered
His help to another, wasting
No time, swinging so swiftly
The traitor's soul abandoned   1770
His body and left it all empty.
And then he turned to a third one,
A brave and noble knight,
And his blow pierced him through,
Blood spurting front   1775
And back; his soul said farewell
To his body, blown away
On a breath. There were many he killed
And maimed: like lightning burning
The air, he beat on whomever   1780
He encountered. When his sword and his spear
Struck, neither shield nor breastplate
Could save them. His companions swung
So freely and well, they scattered
Blood and brains all over.   1785
And the other loyal knights
Cut and sliced the traitors

Like a mob of confused peasants.
They planted so many corpses
In those fields, and labored so long   1790
And hard, that well before dawn
The battle became such a rout
That bodies choked the river
For a full fifteen miles.
Count Angrès left his flag   1795
On the field, and fled, taking
Seven close companions
With him. He headed straight
For the castle by a secret path
So well hidden he was sure   1800
No one knew it existed.
But Alexander, watching
Closely, had seen them fleeing
The field of battle, and thought
He might be able to catch them   1805
If he could slip away unnoticed.
But before he reached the valley
He saw, behind him, coming
Down a path, a group
Of knights, thirty in all,   1810
Of whom six were Greek, and twenty-
Four were Welsh, following
Along, but not too close,
Just in case they were needed.
And seeing them he stopped,   1815
And waited, carefully watching
The fleeing traitors' path
As they came to the castle and went in.
And then he thought of a bold

Plan, exceedingly dangerous   1820
But just as wonderfully clever.
And as soon as the details were clear
In his mind, he rode back to the others,
Greeted them, and said, "Gentlemen,
Let me tell you plainly: if you value   1825
My friendship, then do exactly
As I say, no matter how foolish
It may seem." They agreed to obey
His instructions without dispute,
Whatever they were. "I want us,"   1830
He said, "to change our insignia.
Let's take the traitors' shields
And spears, lying all over.
And then we'll head for the castle
And they'll think we belong there, they'll take us   1835
For men like themselves, and no matter
What happens later they'll open
The gates and let us in.
And how will we pay them back?
We'll kill or capture them all,   1840
If our Lord in heaven is willing.
Hear me: Anyone here
Who's reluctant to try this has lost
My friendship for the rest of my life!"
           They were all happy to agree.   1845
They collected shields from the corpses
And were quickly equipped and ready.
The castle defenders, high
On the tower and along the walls,
Recognized their shields   1850
And thought them traitors, never

Thinking there might be a trap
Hidden behind those shields.
The gates were swung wide open
And the Greeks and Welshmen went in.   1855
The trap had been easily sprung,
For no one demanded a password
Or said a single word.
They entered the castle quietly,
Carefully acting like beaten   1860
Men, dragging their spears,
Slumping forward on their shields,
And looking deeply downcast.
Allowed wherever they wanted
To go, they rode past   1865
All three walls. They saw, up above,
Soldiers and knights too numerous
To count, along with the castle's
Lord. But except for eight
Who had just returned from battle,   1870
They were all unarmed. The eight
Who wore armor had put down their weapons
And were starting to take off their mail shirts—
But they might have been a bit hasty,
For the Greeks dropped their pretense   1875
And, spurring their horses, rode
Right at the traitors' ranks,
Standing tall in the stirrups
And striking tremendous blows
That killed thirty-one traitors   1880
Before the defenders could act.
They were stunned and confused, screaming
"Treachery! We're betrayed!" But the Greeks

And Welshmen were unconcerned,
For facing a disarmed enemy   1885
Their swords could do good work,
And even of those they'd found
With weapons in their hands and armor
On their backs, they'd quickly taken
Good care of three, after   1890
Which, seeing the first ones
Fall, the remaining five
Surrendered and were left alive.
And then Count Angrès
Came dashing up and, as everyone   1895
Watched, struck Macedor
On his golden shield, killing him,
And the Greek fell to the ground.
And Alexander was furious,
Seeing his comrade killed: 1900
Wild anger overwhelmed him,
But instead of making him weaker
It doubled his strength and courage,
And he struck at the count so fiercely
That his spear shattered. Had he   1905
Been able, he would have avenged
His friend on the spot. But the count
Proved himself an exceedingly
Strong and brave and well-trained
Knight, one who might   1910
Have been the best of his time,
Had he not been a cruel traitor.
He gave the Greek so violent
A blow, in return, that his lance
Cracked, broke into bits,   1915

And all that was left were splinters.
But both shields held, and neither
Man was shaken or hurt,
Both bending about
As much as a rock, for both   1920
Were strong and well-built. But the count's
Position was worse, for he
Was clearly in the wrong, and knew it.
Each wildly angry
At the other, both without   1925
Their broken lances, they drew
Their swords and continued the battle.
But neither could gain the advantage:
The combat between these two
Strong fighters might have gone on   1930
And on, and ended who
Knows how, but it had to be stopped,
For the count couldn't afford to linger,
Seeing all around him
The corpses of his men, caught   1935
By surprise, unarmed. Those
Who'd survived were being pursued
Without mercy, cut and hacked
To pieces, their master cursed
As a traitor. Hearing these cries,   1940
The count turned and ran
To his tower, and his men ran after,
With the Greeks and Welshmen hot
On their heels, and of those they caught
One, and only one,   1945
Made his escape. They butchered
So many, hewing and slashing,

That no more than seven in all
Got to safety. But even
Then, when they reached the entrance,   1950
They were forced to stop and fight,
For those who pursued them were so close
Behind they could have entered
The tower, were the way not blocked.
The traitors fought bravely,   1955
Aided by reinforcements
Who had armed themselves in the valley
Below. Nabunal,
A wise Greek, counseled
That the gate to the fortress be barred,   1960
So that those who had carelessly, lazily,
Stayed too long in the town
Could be kept from joining the others.
The tower, up on a height,
Had only one entrance: if they plugged   1965
That opening, too, the count's
Men could never hurt them.
So Nabunal said, and urged them
To listen, that twenty men
Should block the outer gate,   1970
Keeping the traitors from mounting
Any sort of offensive,
For they would surely injure
Arthur's men, if they could.
Twenty knights could guard   1975
The gate, while ten attacked
The tower door, so the count
Could not close it from inside. They accepted
This advice: ten remained

Attacking the tower door,   1980
And twenty rode to the gate,
Arriving barely in time,
For a troop of traitors came up,
Ready and eager to fight,
And with them were many archers   1985
And soldiers of different sorts,
Armed to the teeth, some
With barbed pikes, some
With Danish axes, and Turkish
Spears and lances, and German   1990
Swords, javelins, and crossbows.
It could have been costly indeed,
And the Greeks might well have retreated,
Had the traitors been able to attack,
But they hadn't come in time.   1995
Nabunal's wise advice
Had allowed the Greeks to head them
Off, and keep them outside.
And seeing they had no choice,
They waited quietly where they were,   2000
For nothing could have been gained
By mounting a futile assault.
Then there arose a wild
Wailing, women and small
Children, the old and the young—   2005
So loud that thunder cracking
The sky could not have been heard.
The Greeks fairly danced with joy,
For now they knew for sure
The count could no longer escape them   2010
And would be their captive. Four

Of the twenty hurried up
On the outer walls, not
With combat in mind but only
To watch that those outside   2015
Employed no machines or other
Devices to invade the castle.
And then the other sixteen
Hurried to join the ten
Fighting at the tower door,   2020
Who were making such progress they'd gotten
Past the door and were now
Inside. Wielding an ax,
His back against a post,
The count was fighting fiercely,   2025
Cutting Greeks in half.
His men clustered around him,
Waging their final combat,
Strong and fearless to the last.
And the Greeks were growing depressed,   2030
For only thirteen were left
Where once there'd been twice as many.
Seeing so many of his men
Dead, Alexander
Was wild with anger, but was careful   2035
To keep his mind on revenge:
He'd found, hanging, a long
And heavy iron bar,
And the rascal he struck, and killed,
Got no help from his helmet   2040
Or mail shirt or shield, but toppled
Over and fell on the ground.
And then he went for the count,

Holding the bar high,
And struck him such a blow   2045
With his potent weapon that the ax
Fell from his enemy's hands,
And the count was so stunned and dazed
That even the wall couldn't have held him
Up, and neither could his feet.   2050
That blow ended the battle:
Alexander leaped
At the count, and held him fast.
Why bother mentioning the others?
It was easy to take them prisoner,   2055
Once they saw the count captured.
Master and men were led
Away in shame and dishonor,
Which they richly deserved. But the Greeks
Out on the castle walls   2060
Had no idea what had happened:
The morning after the battle
They came and found their comrades'
Shields lying among
The corpses, and wept for their lord   2065
(Though their tears were not needed), for they knew
Which shield was his. They threw themselves
Down on that shield, declaring
They'd lived too long. Cornin
And Nerice fainted, and when   2070
They awoke again, Cornin
And Acoridome cursed their lives;
Tears came rolling out
Their eyes, and down to their chests;
Life and pleasure alike   2075

Seemed worthless; Parmenides
Especially tore and ripped
At his hair. All of them wept
For their lord as never before
In their lives. But all for nothing: 2080
The body they'd found and thought
Was his belonged to somebody
Else. And they wept yet again,
Finding other shields
And thinking their friends were all dead.   2085
They fell on the bodies and wailed,
But the shields were telling them lies,
For only one was dead,
And his name was Neriolis.
They had every right to mourn him,   2090
If only they'd known the truth.
But they wept and wailed for the others
Quite as much as for him.
So they carried the corpses off,
Though only one was theirs: 2095
Like men in a dream, believing
That what they're dreaming is real,
They allowed the shields to fool them
And accepted lies for truth.
It was only the shields, nothing more.   2100
So they carried the corpses back
To their tents, where many of Arthur's
Men were grieving for their dead.
Yet seeing the Greeks in mourning,
The rest of the army was silent.   2105
A great crowd gathered.
Hearing them mourn her beloved,

Sordamour believed
She'd been born unlucky. Her pain
And torment turned her pale   2110
As a corpse, but what hurt the most
Was not being able to show
Her sorrow openly. She did not
Dare, but kept it hidden
In her heart. But anyone could   2115
Have seen it, had they cared to read
From her face and her body the pain
She was carrying inside. But so many
In Arthur's army were mourning,
Weeping in their own distress,   2120
That no one was concerned for anyone
Else. They cried for themselves,
For family and friends who'd been killed
And maimed, and carried away
By the river. They wept for their own   2125
Losses, sorrowful and bitter.
Sons wept for their fathers,
Fathers wept for their sons,
Brothers for brothers, uncles
For nephews, cousins for cousins: 2130
Everywhere people were mourning
Fathers and brothers and friends.
But the loudest wailing of all
Belonged to the Greeks—for whom,
Had they known it, delight was waiting: 2135
So often the deepest sorrow
Suddenly turns to joy.
          But as the Greeks outside
The castle mourned, those inside

Sought for a way to let it   2140
Be known what joy was waiting.
They disarmed and tied their prisoners,
Who begged to be beheaded at once,
But their captors refused them this kindness,
Saying they'd keep them alive   2145
For the king: Arthur alone
Would decide what sort of punishment
Their treason deserved. With all
Their prisoners disarmed, the Greeks
Marched them to open windows,   2150
So the traitors below could see.
It was not a joyous sight:
Beholding their lord a captive
Was not particularly pleasing.
Then Alexander appeared   2155
And swore, by God and the saints
In heaven, he'd kill the prisoners
One by one, on the spot,
Unless they surrendered themselves
To the king before he could take them.   2160
"Go!" he said. "I command you!
Hurry to my lord the king,
And throw yourselves on his mercy.
Except for the count, none of you
Deserves death. No one   2165
Will be dismembered or killed
If you offer yourselves to the king.
Only the king's forgiveness
Can save you from death: nothing
Else can guarantee   2170
Either your lives or your bodies.

Disarm yourselves at once
And go in search of the king,
Tell him that Alexander
Told you to say he'd sent you.   2175
You won't be wasting your time:
My lord the king will forget
His anger, and pardon you all.
He's a man of grace and forgiveness.
Any other path   2180
Will lead you straight to the grave,
And I'll not regret your deaths."
They listened, and understood,
And believed, and headed for the king's
Tent, and fell on their knees.   2185
There wasn't a man among them
Who didn't do as he'd said.
The king and his knights mounted
Their horses and raced to the castle,
Not wasting a moment. Descending   2190
From the tower, Alexander went
To meet the delighted king,
To whom he delivered the count,
His prisoner. And the king acted
Swiftly, heaping praise   2195
On the Greek; everyone joined
In a flood of congratulations.
The whole army rejoiced:
The sorrow they'd all been feeling
Gave way to delight. But no one   2200
Was happier—for no one could
Have been happier—than the Greeks! Arthur
Gave the rich, incredibly

Costly cup to Alexander,
Assuring him that nothing he owned,   2205
Except the queen's crown,
Was worth as much, but whatever
Else he might want would be his.
But Alexander didn't dare
Request what he longed for most,   2210
His beloved's hand, though he knew
The king would grant it. He was too
Afraid of her displeasure,
Though her heart would have filled with joy,
Knowing he'd rather lament   2215
Without her than have her against
Her will. So he asked the king
To let him wait; he would try
To learn what she wanted. But he did
Not wait to accept the cup;   2220
He asked for no delay.
And later he brought the cup
To my lord Gawain, and begged him
To take it as a token of friendship,
And one he'd labored to acquire.   2225
    When Sordamour heard of her beloved's
Success, her pleasure and delight
Were immense. Learning that he
Was still alive brought her
Such joy that no trace of sorrow   2230
Remained in her heart. And yet,
When he failed to appear at his usual
Time, the hours hung heavy.
She'd have what she wanted, soon
Enough, for both their desires   2235

Pointed in the same direction.
But Alexander was obliged
To wait for even a glance
From those eyes he longed to see.
He'd rather have come to the queen's   2240
Tent at once, but other
Matters detained him. It seemed
Impossible to wait any longer;
The very first moment he could,
He ran to the queen's tent.   2245
Knowing exactly how he felt,
The queen greeted him; he'd said
Not a word, but she'd seen everything,
She understood it all.
She gave him a warm welcome,   2250
Letting him know her pleasure;
Well aware of why
He was there and what he had come for,
She summoned Sordamour.
The three of them sat together,   2255
Away from the others, talking.
Having no doubt that the girl
Loved the Greek, and the Greek loved the girl,
And their love was deep, and shared,
And believing as she did that no one   2260
Would be better for Sordamour,
The queen was determined to help,
And began the conversation.
Seated between them, she steered
Their talk along useful lines: 2265
"Alexander," she said,
"Love can be worse than hate,

If it hurts and destroys the beloved.
Lovers don't know what they're doing
When they hide their love from each other.   2270
Love has its painful aspects;
It can turn your life upside down:
Unless you begin it bravely,
The end can be terribly hard.
It's said that the very first step   2275
Is the worst—crossing the threshold.
So let me teach you Love's lessons,
For believe me, I know you're in pain.
Let me enroll you in his school—
And be careful to hide nothing,   2280
For I know quite well, from watching
Both your faces, that here
Are two hearts beating as one.
So stop this silly concealment!
What dangerous folly, keeping   2285
Your thoughts from one another:
What you don't say is killing
You both. Love will be
Your murderer. Don't let your love
Lead you or compel you. Let the bonds   2290
Of marriage and honor bind you
And hold you together, and thus,
It seems to me, your love
Can be strong and lasting. So let me
Tell you: if you both agree,   2295
If you both want it, I propose
To arrange this marriage." After
The queen had spoken her mind,
Alexander replied: "My lady,"

He said, "there's nothing I can say   2300
To defend myself; I agree
With every word. I've no
Desire to be free of Love:
I hope to serve it forever.
Your words delight me; I thank you,   2305
My lady, for speaking them. And since
You know my wishes so well,
There's no reason to hide them.
If I'd had the courage, I'd have spoken
For myself, and long ago: 2310
Silence has been painful. Still,
It may well be that this girl
Has no interest in making me hers
Or letting herself be mine.
But all the same, even   2315
If she does not want me, I am hers."
Sordamour trembled at these words;
She had no intention of refusing,
And her heart silently spoke
For her, in her voice and her face,   2320
As, shaking, she consented.
Neither her heart nor her will
Nor her body objected in any
Way to what the queen
Had asked them to do: indeed,   2325
It gave her the greatest pleasure.
The queen embraced them both,
And gave each the gift of the other,
Saying, with a smile, "Alexander,
Your beloved's body is yours: 2330
You already own her heart.

No matter who grumbles or groans,
I declare you already married:
A wife for her husband, a husband
For his wife!" It was done, they belonged   2335
To each other, they were one. The very
Same day, as my lord Gawain
And the king agreed, their wedding
Was celebrated at Windsor.
No one, I think, could truly   2340
Describe the rich display,
The pleasure, the food, the delight,
And since whatever I write
Can't be enough, or please
The whole world, I'll waste no words   2345
And keep to the narrow path.
        That day, in Windsor, Alexander
Experienced all the honor
And joy he could ever have wanted.
There were three honors, which were three   2350
Joys: the castle he was given
Was one; another was King Arthur's
Promise, when the war was over,
Of the very best kingdom in Wales—
He'd be king in his castle, that day;   2355
But the third was the greatest of all,
For he'd captured his beloved as queen
For the chessboard on which he'd be king.
Three months later, the new
Wife found herself growing   2360
Grain from her husband's seed,
And she brought that fruit to harvest.
That seed was the start of a human

Being, and the fruit, of course,
Was a child—the loveliest infant   2365
Anyone had ever seen.
They named the baby Cligès.
And this story was written down
In memory of Cligès, its hero.
Soon you'll hear me tell   2370
How he grew, became
A knight and won himself
Fame and honor. In the meantime,
In Constantinople, the emperor
Who ruled Greece came   2375
To the end of his life. He died,
As all of us have to die
When our time has come. But before
He took his last breath, he called
Together the noblest lords   2380
Of his realm, so Alexander
Could be sent for, in far-off England
Where he'd chosen to live. The messengers
Sailed away from Greece
On their long voyage, but a sudden   2385
Storm surprised them, sank
Their ship and killed them all,
Except for a single traitor,
Who as it happened preferred
Prince Alis to his older brother.   2390
Delivered safely from the sea,
He turned and went back to Greece,
Saying the storm had struck them
On the way back from Britain,
And all the others had drowned,   2395

Including Alexander, their lord.
He was the only survivor;
Disaster had taken the rest.
They believed his lies; no one
Challenged his story. With nothing   2400
Further, they made Alis
Their king, and crowned him at once.
But not long after, the news
Was brought to Alexander:
His younger brother was the emperor.   2405
He quickly took leave of Arthur,
Unwilling simply to surrender
His land to his younger brother.
The king made no objection,
But offered to send with him   2410
So many Welsh and Scots
And Cornish soldiers that his brother
Wouldn't dare stand against him,
When he saw the army he'd brought.
So Alexander, had   2415
He pleased, could have returned
In force, but he wanted no carnage,
Hoping his brother would acknowledge
Truth and right, and step down.
All he took were forty   2420
Knights, and his wife and son,
Whom he loved so dearly that he couldn't
Leave them behind. They set sail
From Shoreham, having paid their respects
And said their farewells to the court.   2425
With the wind in its sails, their ship
Bounded across the sea

Like a stag. In less than a month,
I believe, they reached Athens,
A strong and wealthy city.   2430
Indeed, the emperor lived
In Athens, to which he had summoned
A vast assemblage of the noblest
Lords of his land. As soon
As they landed, Alexander   2435
Sent an envoy to see
What sort of welcome he would have:
Would they acknowledge him emperor
Or would he be opposed?
The man he chose for this mission   2440
Was a wise and polished knight;
His name was Acorionde.
Born in Athens, rich
And eloquent, he was sure
To be well received. His family   2445
Bore an ancient, noble
Title, passed from father
To son, and he was its heir.
Learning that Emperor Alis
Was indeed in Athens, he resolved   2450
In the name of Alexander,
His brother and lord, to contest
The crown, for Alis had taken it
Wrongly and broken the law.
He went directly to the palace,   2455
Where many knew him and gave
Him greetings, but he neither answered
Nor spoke to those who welcomed him,
Unsure, as yet, how

They would welcome and what they might do   2460
For their rightful ruler and lord.
Proceeding straight to the emperor,
Not bowing, not giving him greeting,
And calling Alis by name,
Not title, he said: "Alis,   2465
I bring you news of your brother,
Whose ship has just arrived
In Athens. This is his message:
He demands his rightful throne,
Expecting neither less   2470
Nor more. Constantinople
Should be his; it belongs to him,
Not you. He seeks no quarrel
Nor sees any reason for argument.
I suggest you surrender a crown   2475
You cannot hold by right;
Return it to him in peace."
      "My very good friend," said Alis,
"How terribly foolish to bring me
A message like this. You can't   2480
Ease the pain of my brother's
Death, for I know he's dead,
And he can't be here in Athens.
Knowing he was alive
Would give me profound pleasure,   2485
But who could believe without seeing?
He's been dead a long time; I regret it.
But I can't believe what you're saying.
Why isn't he here, if alive?
He knows I'd give him an enormous   2490
Part of my realm. What a fool

He'd be, to stand against me!
He knows he'd do well, in my service.
But the empire and crown are mine,
And no one will take them away."   2495
Hearing the emperor's response,
The messenger knew it was wrong,
And felt not the slightest fear
At speaking his mind. "Alis,"
He said, "may God strike me   2500
Dead, but this won't do.
In your brother's name I defy you!
And in his name, as I must,
I call on everyone here
To leave you and follow their rightful   2505
Ruler, as they should and must:
The throne belongs to him.
And now we'll see who is loyal!"
And speaking these words, he left.
And the emperor summoned those   2510
He trusted most, seeking
Their counsel. If he chose to defy
His brother, he asked, could he count
On their support? Would they promise
Not to aid Alexander?   2515
And so he went from man
To man, but not a single
One advised him to fight.
They urged him, instead, to remember
The war that Polynices   2520
Waged with his brother Etocles;
Both sons of the very same parents,
They ended by killing each other.

"And so it might happen to you,
If he wishes to fight; you   2525
And the land could both be destroyed."
They advised Alis to seek
Some reasonable, lawful peace,
With no one asking too much.
Alis understood that he either   2530
Decided for peace with his brother
Or all his barons would leave him,
And declared that any terms
They suggested would prove acceptable,
Provided only that whatever   2535
Happened he had to insist
On keeping the crown. So he sent
His chief of staff with the message
That Alexander was welcome
To rule the entire country,   2540
But the title of emperor should stay
Where it was, and the crown, and all
The respect and honor. These
Were the terms, he said, on which
They could settle their dispute. And when   2545
These terms and conditions were explained
To Alexander, he
And his men mounted their horses
And rode into Athens. The people
Received them with expressions of joy,   2550
But Alexander was not
Entirely pleased that his brother
Was keeping the title and his crown,
So he made Alis promise
He'd never marry, and after   2555

Him both title and crown
Would go to Cligès. Alis
Gave his word. And thus
The brothers made their peace.
Each swore to these terms,   2560
The younger brother pledging
That as long as he lived he would never
Marry. Agreement was reached,
The brothers remained friends,
And all the barons were delighted.   2565
Alis was still the emperor,
But affairs of state, little
Or large, came to his brother,
Whose orders were always obeyed,
And nothing was done without them.   2570
Alis's portion was simply
The name of emperor, and not much
Else. It was Alexander
Who was served and loved, and where love
Didn't work, fear was sufficient.   2575
Whichever he chose to use,
The whole empire was his
To command. But the power of Death
Makes no distinctions between weak
And strong: we all must die.   2580
And Alexander was dying:
An illness nothing could cure
Had him in its grip. But before
Death could carry him off,
He called for his son, and said,   2585
"My dear Cligès, you'll never
Know how much you're worth —

In strength or courage or virtue —
Until you've tested yourself
At King Arthur's court, along with   2590
The company of Bretons and English.
If the paths of adventure lead you
There, let no one know
Your name, or your father's, until
You've measured yourself against   2595
The best of Arthur's knights.
Remember my words. And if ever
The chance comes to test
Yourself with Gawain, your uncle,
Take it, I beg you. Remember."   2600
Having given his son this counsel,
He lived only a very
Short while. And Sordamour,
Too sorrowful to live, died
With him. Alis and Cligès   2605
Mourned for a time, as they should,
But then they gave up grieving:
Grief should never be cherished,
For it leads to nothing good.
So their sorrow dwindled away.   2610
And then, for some years, the emperor
Held to his word, refusing
To take a wife. But no
Court in all the world
Can ever be free of bad   2615
Advice, and the barons who accept
Such evil counsel are often
Led astray, lost
To the ways of loyal duty.

There were many surrounding the emperor 2620
Who came to him, bearing counsel.
Over and over they urged him
To take a wife; they wheedled
And coaxed, day after day,
Pressing so long and hard 2625
That, finally, their endless arguments
Persuaded him to break his pledge
And do what they wanted, provided,
However, that the future empress
Of Constantinople must be noble, 2630
Prudent, beautiful, and gracious.
At this the barons declared
They were ready, then and there,
To travel to Germany and seek
That emperor's daughter for their queen. 2635
This was the princess they'd chosen
Both because her father
Was a powerful ruler, and rich,
But also because the girl
Was said to be so charming, 2640
So lovely, that no one in the Christian
World could match her beauty.
The emperor endorsed their proposal,
And they went on their way, well
Equipped, riding like gentlemen, 2645
Into Germany. They found
The emperor at Regensburg,
And asked his oldest daughter's
Hand for Emperor Alis.
The emperor could not have been happier, 2650
Agreeing at once to give them

His daughter, for this was a noble
Match that enhanced his prestige.
However, he told them, he'd promised
The girl to the duke of Saxony,   2655
So he couldn't allow the marriage
Unless Alis came
To his empire with a mighty army
And safely escorted the girl,
For without such force the duke   2660
Could stop him from taking her with him.
Having heard the emperor's response,
The messengers took their leave
And returned home. They came
To Emperor Alis and told him   2665
The answer they'd been given.
The emperor selected the best
And most proven of all his knights,
The strongest and bravest he could find,
And with them he took, as well,   2670
The nephew on whose account
He had vowed never to marry—
A pledge he would no longer honor,
If he made his way to Cologne.
        So the emperor's army began   2675
Its march from Greece to Germany.
No censure, and no reproach,
Would keep Alis from marrying;
But his honor would surely suffer.
The army came straight toward Cologne,   2680
Where the emperor and much of his court
Had convened for a German celebration.
And then Alis's men

Reached the gates of the city:
So many Greeks and Germans   2685
Had come to Cologne that they lodged
For forty miles all around.
The crowds were immense, and so
Was the emperors' mutual delight,
Finally meeting each other   2690
In person. The assembly of barons
Was held in the huge hall
Of the palace, and the German emperor
Promptly summoned his daughter
To that hall. There was no delay   2695
In her coming, she appeared at the palace
At once, and proved to be
So beautiful, so shapely a girl,
It seemed that God Himself
Had made her, working hard   2700
To astonish the world. But the hand
That shaped her never formed
A man who could frame such beauty
In words: whatever we
Might say, she was lovelier still.   2705
Her name was Fenice—rightly
So, it seems to me,
For just as the phoenix is the loveliest
Bird of all, unequaled
By any other, just so   2710
Fenice was the loveliest of ladies,
Her beauty unmatched, so wondrous
A miracle that, having achieved it,
Clearly Nature could never
Hope to achieve it again.   2715

Knowing I can't describe her
In words, I won't attempt
To tell you of her arms, her body,
Her head, her hands: stretch
My life to a thousand years,   2720
And double my talent each day,
And still I would always fail.
Why should I try, well
Aware that no matter how hard
I worked, and what skill I employed,   2725
All my effort would be wasted.
So: the girl hurried
To the palace, her head uncovered,
No veil across her face,
And her beauty glowed with a jewel-like   2730
Light that lit the palace
Brighter than four burning
Lamps. And there was Cligès,
With the emperor, his uncle; he'd removed
His cloak. The day was cloudy,   2735
But so much beauty shone
From him, and from the girl,
It was as if the clear,
Radiant morning sun
Had beamed its gleaming rays   2740
Across the palace. His
Is a beauty I can try to describe
In a very few words: he'd reached
The perfect flower of his youth,
Close to the age of fifteen   2745
And already far exceeding
Even the charm and beauty

Of Narcissus, who leaning down
In the shade of an elm tree saw
His own reflection in the water   2750
And loved it so much, they say,
That he died, for fear he couldn't keep it.
Narcissus was lovely, but not
Very bright; Cligès was finer,
As gold is worth more than copper—   2755
And I could say more, but I won't.
His hair looked as if
It were gold, and his face a fresh rose;
His nose was well made, and his mouth;
His height, and his bearing, were so fine   2760
That, plainly, Nature had sought
To blend in one man each
Of the blessings usually given
To many. She'd granted her gifts
With so free a hand that a single   2765
Person possessed them all.
And thus Cligès, lovely
And prudent, generous and strong.
He was perfect wood under perfect
Bark; a better swordsman   2770
And archer than Tristan, King Mark's
Nephew; he trained hawks better,
And hounds. He lacked nothing.
In all his loveliness, he stood
Before his uncle the emperor,   2775
And those who had never met him
Stared without restraint,
Exactly as those who had never
Seen the girl were astonished

At so much loveliness. But Cligès's   2780
Covert look of love,
A swift movement of his eyes
In her direction, and quickly
Back, was fashioned with such
Discretion that no one could think him   2785
A fool—yet a longing look,
And one the girl returned,
Though no one was aware.
And what they exchanged were loving
Looks, not sly or deceitful.   2790
She savored the moment, and would
Have relished it even more
Had she known what manner of man
He was; all she could see
Was his beauty, and she knew she ought   2795
To love someone so lovely
And not love anyone else.
Their hearts followed their eyes
In a silent exchange of vows.
Vows? They gave themselves!   2800
Gave? No, no, that's a lie,
For no one can give his heart.
I need to say this differently.
I don't agree with those
Who say two hearts become one—   2805
That's false and impossible; a single
Body can't have two hearts;
Even if two were joined
Together, it wouldn't be real.
But if you'll listen for a moment,   2810
I think I can tell you exactly

How two hearts can be one,
Without physically joining.
They're one and the same because
What each one wants is sensed   2815
And felt by the other: that's all.
They want the same thing and want it
So much that we say—or some of us
Do—that instead of one heart
Each possesses two,   2820
Though a single heart can't be
In two bodies. And yet two hearts
Can share a single desire,
Much as many different
Voices can sing the very   2825
Same song: the comparison proves
A single body can't have
Two hearts. Consider that settled.
No matter that one heart knows
What the other wants, and wants it,   2830
Too, they're still separate,
Just as voices singing
Together are joined, in a sense,
But aren't a single voice;
No body can have two hearts.   2835
          I've said all I need say:
Another task overtakes me.
I need to tell you more
Of the beautiful girl and Cligès.
You're about to hear of the duke   2840
Of Saxony, who sent one
Of his nephews, a very young man,
To Cologne, to inform the emperor

That his uncle the duke wanted him,
Not to wait for some formal   2845
Truce, but to send him the girl
At once, for anyone else
Who thought to take her wouldn't find
The path open and free
But very effectively defended: 2850
He meant to have the girl.
The young man delivered his message
Well, without pride or insolence,
But no one would answer him, neither
Knight nor emperor, and seeing them   2855
Silent, one and all,
Disdaining his words and his presence,
He turned his back and left
The court. But before he departed,
Too young to know better, he suddenly   2860
Challenged Cligès to combat.
The knights mounted their horses,
Equally divided, three hundred
On one side, the same on the other.
No one was left in the palace   2865
Hall, courtiers and ladies
Hurrying out onto balconies,
Standing at windows, climbing
Battlements, the better to see
Those engaged in the tournament.   2870
Even the girl who'd lost
Her own will, tamed as she was
By Love, ascended to watch.
She sat near a window, and much
Enjoyed the view, well able   2875

To see the one who'd captured
Her heart. She felt no desire
To take it back, for she loved
Only him, and forever,
Despite not knowing his name,   2880
Or who his parents might be,
Or what his rank. Nor would it
Be proper to ask him. She waited,
Eager to hear such things,
Which would fill her heart with joy.   2885
Staring through the window
She watched the shields, shining
With gold, and those who carried them,
Playing at war. But both
Her eyes and her thoughts were always   2890
Fixed, and wandered nowhere
Else: she watched Cligès
In combat, following him
Wherever he went. And waging
This open, public game   2895
Of war, he strove to do well,
So she might hear it said
How brave and skillful he was—
And, in any case, of course
She was sure to praise his prowess.   2900
The duke's nephew was busy
Smashing spears and making
Greeks uncomfortable, which annoyed
Cligès, who buckled his stirrups
Tighter and rode straight at him,   2905
Striking so fiercely that the duke's
Nephew, despite his best efforts,

Was knocked out of his saddle;
There was great excitement, as he rose
From the ground. He climbed on his horse,   2910
Resolved to avenge his dishonor,
But all too often planning
Revenge adds to your shame.
He galloped back at Cligès,
Who lowered his lance and struck   2915
So hard that once again
The youngster tumbled to the ground.
And now his shame was doubled,
And the knights on his side were unhappy,
Suddenly aware the rewards   2920
Of honor would not be theirs,
For none of them were strong
Enough to stay in their saddles
If Cligès attacked them. And the Germans
And Greeks were delighted, seeing   2925
Their side controlling the battle;
Attacking hard, they forced
The enemy into total retreat,
Then chased after them, hurling
Insults, and caught them at a river   2930
Bank, and made them dive
For their baths. Cligès and his comrades
Dunked them down in the deepest
Water, the duke's nephew
And the others with him, until shamed   2935
And miserable they fled the field,
Beaten. Cligès rode joyfully
Back, hailed as the best
On either side; he went

To a door near where she   2940
Was sitting; she made him pay
The toll of a tender glance,
Which she returned as their eyes
Met, thus sealing their mutual
Conquest. Every Greek   2945
And every German old
Enough to speak was saying:
"My Lord, who can this young man
Be, of such flowering beauty?
God, how has it happened   2950
That he's won himself such fame?"
They all were asking each other:
"Who is this youngster? Who is he?"
And in the end everyone
Learned the truth—the young man's   2955
Name, and his father's, and the solemn
Promise made and sworn to
By the emperor. The talk was so
Widespread, so universal
And public, that it came to the ears   2960
Of her whose heart was delighted,
Hearing it, for she could not say,
Now, that Love had made her
A fool; she could not complain,
For the lover Love had found her   2965
Was the noblest, most gracious, bravest,
And loveliest man in the world.
And still, she'd been promised in marriage
To a man who could not please her.
She felt tormented, anguished: 2970
To whom could she tell her secret,

Whisper her true love's name?
Awake and asleep, she thought
Of him, and the constant fretting
Drained the color from her face: 2975
It was no secret to anyone
Who looked, and saw what she'd lost,
That she wanted something she didn't
Have. She played less,
And laughed less, and enjoyed   2980
Less, but hid and denied
Everything, when asked what was wrong.
Her governess, Thessala,
Who had been her childhood nurse,
Was skilled in the art of magic,   2985
For she had been born in Thessaly,
Where diabolical lore
Is known, and taught, and practiced.
Thessalian women are learned
In witchcraft and charms and enchantments.   2990
Seeing the pale, discolored
Face that Love's rule
Had produced, she asked the girl,
In private: "Oh God, have you
Been bewitched, my dear sweet girl?   2995
Your complexion's gone all wrong.
I can't help asking what's happened.
Tell me, if you know,
Where you feel this the most.
If anyone can cure you,   3000
Surely it's me; I know
Exactly how to treat you.
I've cured people of dropsy;

I know what to do with arthritis,
Asthma, pneumonia, and quinsy;   3005
I know urine and the pulse
So well you'll need no other
Physician. And I think I can claim
Such knowledge of tried and tested
Charms and enchantments that Medea   3010
Herself knew less. I've never
Spoken a word of all this,
Though I've been your nurse all your life.
But don't be angry: I'd still
Be careful to say nothing   3015
If I hadn't seen so clearly
That some great sickness has attacked you
And you badly need my help.
My sweet young lady, tell me
What's wrong; that would be wise,   3020
Believe me. Let me help you
Before this goes too far.
Caring for you is the task
Your father assigned me, and you've stayed
Well, I've done as he wanted.   3025
But all my work will be wasted
If I can't cure you now.
Be careful, don't keep things from me:
Is this an illness or something
Different?" The girl did not dare   3030
Disclose the strength of her feelings,
Afraid she might be blamed
Or scolded, and worried the woman
Might try to change her mind.
But having heard how highly   3035

The governess valued her magical
Skills, her knowledge of charms,
Enchantments, and potions, she told her
Why she was pale and her complexion
Disordered, but only after   3040
Making the woman swear
She'd forever keep the secret
And not seek to argue her out
Of love. "Governess, I hadn't
Thought I was sick, I felt   3045
No pain. But now I'm not sure.
There's only one thing I think of,
And it's making me ill. I'm frightened.
But how can you know, without
Experience, what's bad or good?   3050
This sickness is different from any
I've known—I'm telling the truth—
It makes me both happy and sad—
It's the most delightful misery!
If a pleasant sickness is really   3055
Possible, I love my suffering
And my sickness is truly my health,
And I don't know why I'm complaining,
For whatever I feel is what
I want to feel. I enjoy it!   3060
Perhaps desire is my sickness,
But it makes me feel so good
That even suffering is sweet;
There's so much pleasure in my pain
That being ill is wonderful.   3065
Thessala, isn't this
A two-faced sickness, making me

Feel so good and so bad?
How can I know if this
Is truly a sickness, or something   3070
Else? Tell me, Thessala:
What is this? And how does it work?
Yet understand, please:
A cure is not what I want.
I cherish this disease."   3075
Knowing the secrets of Love,
And its hidden ways, Thessala
Saw at once that the girl's
Torments were the pangs of love.
The fact that she found her illness   3080
Sweet was proof certain,
For every other disease
Is bitter; the only exception
Is love. Love can transform
Its special bitterness to sweetness   3085
And delight, then transform it back.
Knowing all this, Thessala
Answered: "I think you know
The name and nature of this sickness
Of yours, and know it well.   3090
The feelings you've been describing
Are signs, are they not, of a sweet
Sadness you find delightful,
And that's the sickness of love,
Born out of joy and sorrow.   3095
So you're in love, I assure you:
For no sickness I know of
Is sweet, except for love.
All other illnesses tend

To be cruel and horrible, but love   3100
Is peaceful and sweet. So you're
In love, that's certain. There's nothing
Wrong with being in love,
But it's very wrong, for careless
Or foolish reasons, to hide   3105
Your heart from me." "Thessala,
Every word you say
Is in vain, unless you convince me
That nothing and no one can make you
Tell a living soul."   3110
"My dear sweet girl, the wind's
More likely to speak than I am,
Unless you tell me to speak.
But let me promise you this:
I'll do whatever I can   3115
To help you; when you have your happiness,
You won't be in doubt whom to thank."
"Thessala, I'd be cured on the spot,
But my father's already promised
My hand, which is more than sad,   3120
It's horrible: the one I want
Is nephew to the one I'm to marry!
If the Emperor Alis takes his pleasure
Of me, I'll have lost all joy
Of my own, there'll be no hope.   3125
I'd sooner be torn apart
Than see Cligès and myself
Relive the love of Tristan
And Iseult, a shameful story
To tell, full of foolishness.   3130
I couldn't accept the life

Iseult was obliged to lead!
Love was her savage enemy,
Giving her body to two men
While her heart belonged to just one.   3135
She never said no to either—
And thus she led her whole life.
That was unstable, irrational
Love, but mine is fixed,
Unchanging: no matter the cost,   3140
Nothing will divide my heart
And body. I'm not a whore,
And I won't be used like a whore.
When I give my heart, I give
My body, and no one else   3145
Will have it. But how can my heart
Give my body to the man
It loves, when my father's given
My hand to someone else?
I can't contradict my father.   3150
If Alis is lord of my body,
And uses it, against my will,
To give it to anyone else
Would be sinful. But Alis can't marry
Unless he breaks his vow,   3155
For unless he wrongs his nephew,
Cligès will be emperor when he dies.
You'd do me an immense service,
Thessala, if you knew some trick
So the man to whom I'm given   3160
And pledged won't have my body.
Do your best, my mistress,
To ensure that Emperor Alis

Fulfills both the promises
He made to Cligès's father: 3165
He'd never marry, and Cligès
Would succeed him. If he marries me,
As he means to, his oaths will be broken.
But how could I treat Cligès
So badly that on my account 3170
He loses the least of the honors
He deserves? I'd rather be buried
Alive! I'll never give birth
To a child who cheats Cligès!
Do this for me, mistress, 3175
And I'll be yours forever!"
Thessala swore she'd prepare
A potion for Emperor Alis
So potent with incantations,
Charms and conjurations, 3180
That as soon as he put the cup
To his lips, and drank, there'd be nothing
More to fear from him:
Even sharing his bed,
The girl would be as safe, 3185
And could feel as sure, as if
A wall had been built between them.
And Thessala explained that Alis
Would have his pleasure, but only
In sleep, in dreams, that would not 3190
Bother the girl: he'd think
Himself awake, he'd think
It was truly happening; for him,
A lying, cheating dream
Would be pleasure and joy. Nor would it 3195

Change; this would last forever;
He'd sleep, and think he was happy.
    Fenice was delighted at this wonderful
Trick, which she praised and admired:
By swearing she meant to work   3200
Such infallible magic, Thessala
Had given her hope. She'd have
What she longed for, in the end, no matter
How long she had to wait.
For how could Cligès object,   3205
Knowing she loved him? A noble
Heart like his could only
Rejoice, seeing her stay
A virgin to preserve his inheritance.
If his was as good, as noble   3210
A nature as she thought, he'd have
To feel compassion and pity.
She trusted and believed in her governess,
And told her everything, and the two
Exchanged pledges and vows   3215
Of silence; to keep their plan
Secret, neither would say
A word. And so they ended
Their talk. The next morning,
Her father sent for the girl.   3220
She came, as he had commanded.
But why describe the scene?
The two emperors were in such
Complete agreement that marriage
Vows were exchanged and courtiers   3225
Began to celebrate
Their joy. But of all the details

You need to know only
What the governess did, endlessly
Brewing and mixing her potions,   3230
Casting her spells and enchantments.
      First she brewed the drink,
Then tempered it, blended it smooth
And even with a host of spices;
She beat it well, and made it   3235
Mellow, then filtered it completely
Clear, neither bitter nor sharp,
Sweetened and beautifully scented
By the herbs and spices she had used.
And once it was ready, just   3240
As the day was drawing to a close,
And the guests were sitting at well-laid
Tables, eager to dine—
But never mind their food.
Thessala needed a device,   3245
A way of presenting her special
Beverage to its intended victim.
There were ten or twelve seated
At the royal table; Cligès
Was serving his uncle Alis.   3250
Watching him work at this courteous
Task, it seemed to Thessala
He labored against himself,
Which made her angry, and sad.
How fitting, she thought, to have   3255
Alis's drink offered
By the person whose pleasure and worth
It would serve. She motioned Cligès
To rise and come to her; he did so,

Asking the governess why   3260
She had called him, and what she wanted.
"My friend," she said, "I wish
To honor the Emperor Alis,
At this wedding banquet, with a wonderful
Drink. By Saint Riquier!   3265
Whether at table or in
His bed, he should drink no other.
He'll love it: I've never tasted
Better, or any so costly.
Be careful, I warn you, that no one   3270
Else drinks a drop,
For there's not much more. And let me
Suggest you keep its origin
Secret: tell him, if he asks,
You found it, by chance, among   3275
The wedding gifts, and tried
Its bouquet, and found the scent
Of its choice spices perfuming
The air, and saw how perfectly
Clear it was, and decided   3280
To pour it into his cup.
Tell him this, if he asks,
And he'll ask no more. Don't think,
Please, there's any need
To feel suspicious: this   3285
Is a clear and healthy drink,
Filled with excellent herbs
And spices. Some day, perhaps,
You'll know for yourself what good
It might do you." Hearing that good   3290
Could come of it, Cligès accepted

The flask and poured the potion
In the emperor's crystal cup,
Thinking no evil thoughts.
Alis trusted his nephew   3295
And drank a mighty draft—
And felt its power at once,
Flowing from his head to his body,
Then rising back to his head
And spreading out all over.   3300
It did him no harm, but it ran
Everywhere. And when it was time
To rise from the table, Alis
Had taken so well to the potion,
And drunk so much, that he fell   3305
Asleep in his bed and slept
The night through, never waking,
For the magic worked so well
That, dead asleep, he felt
Awake. And thus he was cheated.   3310
Bishops and abbots had thronged
Around the bed, and blessed it,
And when it was time to sleep
Alis had gone to bed,
As he should, with his new young wife.   3315
As he should? I've told you a lie!
He neither kissed her nor touched her,
Though he lay all night at her side.
The girl trembled with fear,
Deeply afraid that the magic   3320
Potion might do no good.
But the emperor had been so thoroughly
Bewitched that he wanted no woman,

Not her and no other, except
In his sleep, taking such pleasure   3325
In his dreams, not knowing them dreams,
That his memory took them for real.
She was still fearful, staying
As far from him as she could,
Trying to keep him away.   3330
But he was soon asleep, and dreaming,
And thinking himself awake,
Taking great pains to be gentle
With the girl he had married, and she
Defending herself against him,   3335
Trying to remain a virgin,
And he was coaxing and calling her
Soft and loving names,
Believing he'd had her but having
Nothing, delighting in nothing,   3340
Kissing and caressing nothing,
Loving nothing, whispering
To no one, seeing and holding
No one, struggling with no one.
Magic that worked so well   3345
And lasted so long was surely
Well made! He had labored in vain,
Believing he'd been successful,
Convinced he'd conquered her fortress
And fallen, proud and exhausted,   3350
On her panting breast. He believed it!
But let me tell you one last
Time: he'd enjoyed no one.
And so it would stay forever,
If he lived to take her away.   3355

But before he had safe possession
I'm afraid there might be some problems:
On the journey back to Greece
He'd have to deal with the duke
To whom she'd been promised, and he'd   3360
Prepared Alis a warm welcome.
Assembling a mighty army,
He was watching all the borders,
And he'd posted spies at her father's
Court, who sent him daily   3365
Reports on who was readying
Troops and equipment, and how long
It would take, and when Alis
Would be leaving, and what route he would take.
Nor did Alis intend   3370
To linger, once he was married:
He left Cologne in good spirits,
And the German emperor went with him,
Along with a good many knights,
For he feared an attack by the duke.   3375
They traveled quickly, reaching
Regensburg before
They camped, setting their tents
In a field along the Danube.
The Greek forces were lodged   3380
Near the Black Forest; not far
Away was the Saxon camp,
Watching and waiting. The duke's
Nephew, leading an advance
Guard, had climbed a hill,   3385
Hoping to gain some advantage
On those they meant to injure.

Watching from their post on high,
They saw Cligès riding
Out with three of the young   3390
Greeks, carrying shields
And spears, intending some sport.
The duke's nephew, longing
To harm them if he could, took two
Companions and quietly, keeping   3395
Low, went down to the valley
And hid themselves in the wood.
The Greeks, suspecting nothing,
Wandered down the valley,
And the duke's nephew came dashing   3400
Out at Cligès, striking
At his back but wounding him only
Slightly, for Cligès alertly
Bent forward, and the spear slipped past.
The wound was hardly serious,   3405
But finding himself in danger
Cligès attacked his attacker
And struck him such a blow
That his spear pierced him straight through
The heart and killed him at once.   3410
The other Saxons, frightened,
Fled into the forest.
Not knowing he'd survived an ambush,
Cligès committed the reckless
Folly of leaving his Greeks   3415
Behind and chasing the fleeing
Attackers, who fled to that part
Of the forest where the duke's army
Was stationed, waiting for their chance

To fall on the Greeks. Cligès   3420
Was all alone, pursuing
The desperate Saxons, who had lost
Their young lord. They ran straight
To the duke himself and told him,
Weeping and sobbing, that his nephew   3425
Was dead, and who had killed him.
The duke was scarcely amused:
He swore in the name of God
And His saints that as long as he knew
His nephew's murderer remained   3430
Alive, nothing in life
Could please him, declaring that whoever
Brought him the murderer's head
Would be his friend forever
And receive a rich reward.   3435
One of his knights swore
To bring him Cligès's head
As a gift, if the Greek would fight him.
Then Cligès, pursuing the Saxons,
Stumbled upon the duke's   3440
Army, and the knight who'd vowed
To kill him saw him coming.
He headed straight for the Greek,
But Cligès had quickly turned back
As soon as he saw the army,   3445
Trying as fast as he could
To rejoin the comrades he'd left
Behind. He could not find them,
For they'd gone back to their camp
To report their adventure. Alis   3450
Immediately ordered Greek

And German knights to their horses,
And the whole army alerted
And ready for war. Meanwhile,
The Saxon knight, well armed,   3455
His helmet laced, came spurring
His horse behind Cligès.
Seeing the Saxon alone,
Cligès, who had never been
A coward or inclined to run   3460
From battle, called out insults,
And the knight, angry and unable
To contain his anger, promptly
Called him a stupid child:
"Boy," he shouted, "now   3465
You'll pay for killing my lord!
All I'll take is your head;
It's the only ransom I want,
And all I need from you.
I'll bring it back to the duke,   3470
In exchange for the nephew you killed.
He'll say it's a very good trade."
He was talking wildly, foaming
At the mouth like a vulgar fool.
"Be careful, fellow," Cligès   3475
Responded. "I'll argue the point,
And you'll get nothing, if it's up
To me." They rushed at each other.
The Saxon missed, but Cligès
Struck him so hard that he   3480
And his horse tumbled in a heap,
The animal falling heavily
And right on top of its master,

Breaking his leg. Cligès
Dismounted, walked across   3485
The soft green grass and disarmed him,
And then, arming himself
With the Saxon's sword, he cut off
The Saxon's head. And when
He'd chopped it off, he mounted   3490
His trophy on the point of his spear.
If he happened to meet the duke
On the field of battle, he said,
He'd offer him this instead
Of the Greek head he'd been promised.   3495
Wearing the Saxon's helmet,
Now, with the Saxon's shield
Hung around his neck,
Cligès climbed up on the Saxon's
Horse, instead of his own   3500
(Letting his own horse roam
As he pleased, to have the pleasure
Of frightening his fellow Greeks),
When suddenly he saw a hundred
Greek and German banners,   3505
And the whole vast army on the move.
A fearful, cruel, and savage
Battle against the Saxons
Was about to begin. Seeing
The emperor's forces arriving,   3510
Cligès headed straight for the Saxons,
And the Germans and Greeks pursued him,
Not knowing who he was,
The emperor Alis convinced
That the head at the end of that Saxon   3515

Lance had belonged to Cligès,
His own nephew. Could anyone
Be surprised by such
A mistake? The emperor's army
Chased him, and Cligès led them   3520
Along, intending to start
The fighting as soon as he reached
The Saxons. But his Saxon armor
And insignia confused them; his trick
Succeeded in making them fools.   3525
The duke himself, seeing him
Riding, his lance at rest,
Cried: "Here comes our knight!
That head he's got on his spear
Must be Cligès! And the Greeks   3530
Are chasing after him! Hurry,
Quickly, we need to help him!"
They came racing toward Cligès,
Who continued to gallop at them,
Bent low behind his shield,   3535
His spear jutting out, bearing
Its head—as brave as Samson,
But not any stronger than an ordinary
Man. Everyone—Saxon,
And Greek, and German—thought   3540
He was dead; his enemies rejoiced,
His friends mourned—but not
For long: dashing straight
At a Saxon, striking him full
In the chest with his spear, adorned   3545
With its head, and rolling him out
Of his saddle, he shouted insults

And defiance: "Now fight, my friends!
You wanted Cligès; he's here!
Now fight, you brave fellows!   3550
No cowards wanted here!
The first round's ours! Cowards
Don't care for that sort of victory!"
Emperor Alis was delighted,
Hearing his nephew's voice   3555
Exhorting them into battle;
But if he rejoiced, the duke
Was stunned, shocked to the core,
For he saw that his cause was lost,
If he couldn't recover the advantage.   3560
He drew his forces into ranks,
And the Greeks and Germans, in good order,
Didn't keep much of a distance,
But spurred their horses and attacked.
Both sides thrust with their spears,   3565
Giving and taking blows
As the way of war demands.
Shields began to shatter,
Lances began to crack;
Straps snapped, stirrups   3570
Broke. Many horses
Were riderless, their masters lying
On the ground. But no matter what happened
Around them, Cligès and the duke
Fought, pointing their spears,   3575
Striking such heavy blows
On each other's shields that their lances,
Strong and well-shaped wood,
Flew apart in splinters.

Cligès was a splendid horseman,   3580
Sitting erect in the saddle,
Not wavering or losing his balance.
In spite of himself, the duke
Was thrown from his saddle, and Cligès
Expected to take him prisoner,   3585
And tried hard to get at him,
But one man alone couldn't take him,
For the Saxons closed around
And led him away from the field.
But Cligès emerged from the battle   3590
Unwounded, with a handsome reward:
He led away the duke's
Horse, whiter than wool
And worth, in a warrior's hands,
The wealth of Roman Octavian—   3595
A pure Arabian steed.
Greeks and Germans alike
Were delighted, seeing him astride
Such a horse, knowing as they did
What a brave and magnificent animal   3600
It was. But though they were quite
Unaware, a trap had been laid
That would soon cost them dear.
A Saxon spy had just
Returned to the duke with joyful   3605
News: "My lord, the Greeks
Have left their tents completely
Unguarded—not a single defender!
And the emperor of Germany, believe me,
My lord, is thinking of nothing   3610
Except the battle. Why fight

For the girl when you can go and take her?
Give me a hundred knights
And I'll fetch you the girl. I know
A secret road, and I'll take   3615
Your men to the camp so quietly
That no one will see them, no one
Will know, until we reach
The tent and take the girl
Without a bit of bloodshed."   3620
       The idea delighted the duke.
He sent a hundred knights
And more to return with the spy,
And their mission was quickly, successfully
Concluded, for they took the girl,   3625
Barely exerting themselves,
And easily led her away.
Emerging from the Greeks' tents,
They chose her an escort of twelve,
And quietly left the camp,   3630
Then sent her off with her escort
While the rest of the raiders rode
Right to the duke, to tell him
How well they'd done their business.
Since she was all he wanted,   3635
He quickly agreed to a truce
With the Greeks, to last till tomorrow.
Once the truce was arranged,
The duke's ambassadors left,
And the Greeks, waiting for nothing   3640
And no one, returned to their tents.
But Cligès had ridden to the top
Of a hill, and stayed there watching,

Though no one noticed; he'd seen
The twelve-man escort galloping   3645
Off, and someone with them.
Hungry for fame and honor,
It seemed to Cligès they wouldn't
Be hurrying away for no reason.
Their haste was important. So he followed.   3650
And the twelve knights saw him
At once, riding on their trail,
And thought, seeing the horse
He was riding, it had to be
The duke. "Let's wait a bit,"   3655
They said. "He's left the army
All alone, wanting to catch up."
It seemed perfectly clear.
So half of the twelve decided
To ride out and greet him, each on his   3660
Own. Cligès had just
Ridden between two mountains,
Down in a valley. Without
Their stopping to wait, he'd never
Have followed their traces or known   3665
Where they were. So six approached him—
An unlucky encounter for them.
And the other six remained
With the girl, ambling slowly
Along. The six who'd come   3670
To greet the duke rode swiftly,
Two by two, through the valley.
And the fastest rider among them
Came straight to the duke (as he thought),
Calling: "God save you, Duke   3675

Of Saxony! We've got the girl.
We took her away from the Greeks.
She's yours, my lord, all yours!"
Hearing and understanding
These shouted words, Cligès   3680
Felt no laughter in his heart,
But a surge of almost insane
Anger. No savage beast,
No lion or tiger or leopard,
Seeing its cubs captured,   3685
Could have roared with wilder fury
Or more excitedly dashed
Into battle, for life without
His beloved was worthless. He'd sooner
Have died than fail in her rescue;   3690
His anger quickened his courage
And filled him with strength. He spurred
The Arabian horse and drove
His spear right through the middle
Of the Saxon's shield, so fierce   3695
A blow, to tell you the truth,
That the point struck to the heart.
Encouraged by this initial success,
Cligès galloped two hundred
Feet, his spurs goading   3700
The Arabian horse along,
Until the next of the Saxons
Reached him; he feared nothing,
Seeing how they came
One at a time, each of them   3705
Riding alone, with no one
To help or support him. He met

The second Saxon, who also
Thought he was giving the duke
Good news, as the first had done.   3710
But pleasure was not what Cligès
Wanted; he wished to hear
No speeches. Piercing him through
With his spear, he pulled it back,
The blood gushed, and soul   3715
And words vanished together.
The third one came, expecting
A warm welcome. He was wrong.
The Arabian horse hit him,
And before he could say a word,   3720
Cligès's lance was six feet
Deep through his body. The fourth one
Suffered so fierce a blow
That he lay unconscious on the ground.
And after the fourth came the fifth,   3725
And after the fifth the sixth—
All dead without resistance,
Unable to open their mouths.
There were six of them left, but he wasn't
Worried, for six were gone   3730
And he thought he could handle the rest.
Indeed, with them out of
The way, danger and dishonor
Were the only gifts he would give
To those who were guarding the girl.   3735
Reaching the others, he attacked
Like a starving wolf leaping
On its prey, tormented by hunger—
And excited by the opportunity

To display his skills as a knight,   3740
And his courage, under the eyes
Of the woman he loved so wildly.
She'd either be rescued, or he'd
Be dead, and she with him,
Dying of fear and despair,   3745
Not knowing how close he was.
A pleasant flick of his spurs
Let Cligès, lance ready, strike
A Saxon, and then another,
One swift assault stretching   3750
Both of them out on the ground
But shattering his wooden spear.
They fell in such pain that neither
Could rise or hope to attack
And hurt him, their wounds far   3755
Too serious. The remaining four,
Furious, came at him at once,
All together, but he neither
Retreated nor trembled, nor leaped
Out of the saddle. Quickly   3760
Unsheathing the sharp steel
Of his sword, he swung it in the name
Of her who awaited his love,
And struck one of the onrushing
Saxons so swiftly and well   3765
That he sliced his head away
From his body, and half of his neck
And shoulder, showing not
The slightest pity. Watching
This battle, however, Fenice   3770
Had no way of knowing who he was.

She could have wished him to be
Cligès but, seeing the danger,
Changed her mind. Yet it made
No difference: a friend whoever   3775
He was, she hoped for success,
Yet feared his death. Cligès
Attacked; the three Saxons resisted,
Hammering so hard on his shield
That it split, but unable to seize him   3780
Or crack the metal of his mail shirt.
But wherever Cligès struck,
Nothing could stand; he smashed
And broke whatever he hit.
He spun faster than a top   3785
Whipped along the ground.
Both pride and the love that bound him
Lent him courage and strength;
He attacked the Saxons so savagely
That all were defeated, killed   3790
Or conquered or maimed, but one
He allowed to escape, for he'd fought
Cligès like an equal, and because
Cligès wanted the duke
To know who had brought him such shame   3795
And sorrow. And before the Saxon
Left, he asked Cligès
To tell him his name, and Cligès
Told him, and the duke was furious,
When he heard. Heavy misfortune   3800
Weighed him down. But Cligès,
Having saved Fenice, had to struggle
With the pangs of love, unable

To confess his feelings, aware
That silence, now, might hurt him   3805
Forever. She, too, held her tongue,
Not saying what her heart felt,
Though this was the time to speak,
To tell each other what they wanted.
But each was afraid of the other,   3810
Not knowing what might be said.
He was afraid she would turn him
Away; she would have said
She loved him, had she known what he'd say.
Their eyes admitted everything,   3815
Opened their hearts to each other,
But eyes alone can't speak.
The look in their eyes was almost
Words, but their mouths were cowards,
Their tongues so tied by love   3820
That speech became impossible.
How easy to understand
Her silence! Girls must be cowards,
Innocent, simple. But he,
Having shown her the courage of which   3825
He was capable, how could he shrink
From her, as from no one else?
Tell me, oh Lord, where girls'
Timidity comes from, their trail,
Fearful, innocent silence?   3830
I feel as if I'm seeing
Hounds fleeing a hare,
Trout chasing after beavers,
Lambs after wolves, pigeons
Pursuing eagles. Or peasants   3835

Their shovels, which earn them their weary
Lives. Or ducks after falcons,
Storks after hawks, minnows
Splashing after pike,
Antelope hunting lions: 3840
The world all upside down!
All the same, I'd like
To explain why, as it seems
To me, the most perfect lovers
Lack the good sense and courage   3845
To speak their minds, though time
And place are perfect for speaking.
      You who are learned in Love
And carefully, faithfully keep
The customs and ways of its court,   3850
Never breaking its laws
No matter what's said or done,
Tell me: have you ever seen
A lover who doesn't tremble
And go pale when Love smiles?   3855
Try to deny it, if you can:
The facts are clear, and I know them.
Whoever *doesn't* tremble
And go pale is as good as senseless—
A thief trying to claim   3860
What can't be rightfully his.
A servant who's unafraid
Of his master doesn't stay in service,
Or even start. A master
Has to be worthy of fear   3865
For a servant to feel it: you steal him
Blind, you trick him and lie,

If he's not. A master's very
Words—not just his commands—
Must make a servant tremble,   3870
And whoever's a servant of Love
Must make him his lord and master;
His mind must be filled with Love, forever
Serving and honoring him, or there's no
Admittance to his court. Love   3875
With no trembling or fear is a fire
Without heat, a sunless day,
Wax without honey, summer
Without flowers, a frostless winter,
A moonless sky, a book   3880
With no letters. My argument runs:
When fear goes, Love
Has disappeared with it.
You need to fear, if you love;
There's no love without it—   3885
But only the fear of not
Being loved, for lovers must be brave.
Thus Cligès was neither mistaken
Nor wrong when he feared his beloved.
And yet, he wouldn't have remained   3890
Silent, he would have declared
His love and asked for hers,
However she took his words,
If she weren't his uncle's wife.
This was a wound that truly   3895
Hurt, for the torments he suffered
Couldn't be eased by speaking.
        Thus they went back to their people,
And whatever words they exchanged

Were not about things that mattered.   3900
Both were mounted on excellent
Horses, which they hurried along.
The Greeks and Germans had been mourning,
The entire army afflicted,
But their tears had all been wasted,   3905
Though the pain and suffering were real,
For Cligès had not been killed.
And they grieved for Fenice, no one
Expecting ever to see her
Again. It was double mourning,   3910
Exceedingly sad and sorrowful.
But neither Cligès nor the girl
Wanted the grief to continue:
They hurried back, and quickly
Transformed sadness to joy.   3915
Happiness reigned, sorrow
Fled, as everyone welcomed
Them home, the whole vast host.
Both the emperors hurried
To greet them, the moment they heard   3920
Cligès and the girl were returning,
And gave them the warmest of welcomes.
All found it hard to wait
While Cligès explained just how
He'd found and rescued the empress.   3925
He told them his tale, and those
Who heard him were amazed, showering
Praises on his courage and skill.
But the duke, in the enemy camp,
Was enraged, swearing he'd challenge   3930
Cligès to combat, if the young man

Dared, and he set the conditions
Thus: if Cligès won,
Alis would be free to leave
In peace, and the girl with him;   3935
And if Cligès—who had done him such terrible
Wrongs—either lost or was killed,
There'd be no truce and no peace:
They'd fight till one side won.
The duke expected to beat   3940
The boy, then fight for the wife
He wanted. His translator (who knew
Both Greek and German) presented
His challenge, explaining the duke's
Terms to the two emperors.   3945
          This messenger spoke his piece
Aloud, in both languages,
So all would understand.
The camp buzzed with discussion,
Everyone sure that God   3950
Did not intend this duel
To take place, and both emperors
Agreed, fearing the result.
But Cligès fell to his knees,
Begging them not to worry: 3955
If anything he'd done had pleased them,
Whatever merit he'd earned
Should let him deserve this combat.
But were he forbidden to fight,
He'd be forced to forswear his uncle's   3960
Service forever. Emperor
Alis, who cherished his nephew
Dearly, as well he should,

Took him by the hand and raised him
From his knees, saying, "Dear nephew,   3965
Seeing you so anxious to fight
Grieves me, for sorrow can follow
On joy. Of course you've pleased me!
But I'm deeply afraid to send you
Into this battle: it seems   3970
To me you're far too young.
And yet, knowing your pride
And courage, I can't refuse you
Anything you ask: only
Your own urgent request   3975
Allows me to let this go forward.
But if my prayers were answered
You'd never accept this challenge."
"My lord," said Cligès, "there's nothing
To discuss. May God confound me   3980
If I wouldn't rather fight
This battle than win the whole world!
I can't understand why
We're waiting. Let's not delay."
The emperor wept with compassion,   3985
Agreeing to the combat, but Cligès
Wept with joy. And many
Others wept as well,
But no delay was allowed:
By nine that morning the duke's   3990
Messenger returned with the news
That the challenge had been accepted,
Exactly as the duke had wanted.
        The duke was convinced, of course,
That Cligès would have no chance: 3995

His death or defeat were certain.
He had himself armed at once.
But Cligès, who was eager to fight,
Was not in the least concerned
That the duke might be stronger, and win.   4000
He asked his uncle to give him
Armor and make him a knight,
And Emperor Alis was glad
To do whatever he wanted,
Seeing how his heart burned   4005
And hungered and thirsted for battle.
Cligès was quickly ready,
Armored from head to foot;
Heavy hearted, the emperor
Buckled his nephew's sword.   4010
And wearing his armor, bearing
His weapons, Cligès was mounted
On his Arabian horse, a shield
Of elephant bone hanging
From his neck, so tough that nothing   4015
Could scratch it, and no paint or color
Would stick. His armor was white,
And his horse and harness were white,
Whiter than the purest snow.
　　　　Cligès and the duke were mounted   4020
And ready. They'd arranged to meet
In the middle of the field. Behind them,
At each of the ends, were their men,
No one carrying sword
Or spear, all solemnly sworn   4025
To abstain, while the battle lasted,
From the slightest sort of active

Assistance for either combatant:
They'd sooner have plucked out an eye!
These were the rules for the battle,   4030
And both were impatient to begin,
Each of them sure the joys
Of victory and glory would be his.
But before a blow could be struck,
The empress, deeply anxious   4035
For Cligès, inspected the field,
Having made up her mind that if he
Died, she would die with him;
No one could stop her from killing
Herself, for life without him   4040
Could give her no pleasure. When all
Who wanted to watch were assembled,
Noble and peasant, young
And old, and the guards were in place,
Cligès and the duke set   4045
Their lances and attacked at once,
Crashing so hard that both
Broke their spears and both
Were spilled out of the saddle
And onto the ground. They jumped   4050
To their feet immediately, neither
Man wounded or hurt,
And went back to fighting, playing
Tunes on each other's helmets,
Which rang from the furious sword blows.   4055
The entire audience was astonished,
Imagining both men's helmets
Consumed with burning fire,
For every leaping swordstroke

Threw off showers of sparks 4060
Like a blacksmith in his forge hammering
Red-hot iron on an anvil.
They offered each other stunning
Strokes, both of them generous,
Both determined to pay back 4065
Blows without delay,
Both spending their combat capital
Freely, not counting pennies,
Not stopping to appraise each other's
Security or calculate interest. 4070
But the duke was wild with anger,
Furious, flaming, that his first
Strokes hadn't settled the matter
And beaten Cligès to the ground.
He swung as hard as he could, 4075
A tremendous stroke that bent
Cligès to one knee. Emperor
Alis was deeply dismayed,
Stunned by the shock of that blow
As if the sword had fallen 4080
On his shield rather than Cligès's.
Fenice, even more frightened,
Could not restrain herself,
But cried, as loud as she possibly
Could, "Oh Holy Mary!" 4085
But those were her only words,
For her voice utterly failed,
And she fainted, falling flat
On her face with her arms stretched
To the side, bruising her forehead. 4090
Two of the emperor's barons

Picked her up and held her
Erect until she returned
To herself. No one could tell
From her face who or what   4095
Had caused her to faint, yet no one
So much as thought of blaming her,
But praised her, instead, for each
And all were convinced she'd have done
The same for them, had they   4100
Been where Cligès now was.
As we know, they were quite mistaken.
Cligès could hear her cry
Perfectly clearly, and her voice
Renewed his courage and strength.   4105
He leapt to his feet and immediately
Ran at the duke, attacking
Fiercely and pressing him hard,
Which left the duke astonished,
For it seemed to him that Cligès   4110
Was fighting stronger and quicker
Now than he'd fought when their combat
Had first begun. Fearing
The young man's assault, he said,
"My boy, by all that's holy,   4115
You're wonderfully brave and skilled!
Except for my nephew's death
I'd rather forget our quarrel,
Make peace with you, concede
That you acted rightly, and never   4120
Meddle in this again."
"Duke," said Cligès, "are you saying
It's better to abandon your rights

When you find you can't enforce them?
When you're forced to choose between   4125
A pair of evils, pick
The lesser. Your nephew was angry
And foolish, attacking me.
But understand: unless
You offer an honorable peace,   4130
I'll kill you, too, if I can."
Thinking Cligès would go on
Growing stronger and stronger,
The duke decided, before
Completely exhausting himself,   4135
It was better to abandon the field
Than to keep pursuing a dangerous
Road to its miserable end.
All the same, he wouldn't
Openly admit the truth.   4140
"My boy," he said, "I can see
You're noble, and brave, and proud,
Though still too young. I have
No doubt I'll beat you or kill you,
If we go on fighting. But how much   4145
Honor can I win, defeating
You? To whom could I boast
Of my victory, fighting a youngster
Like you? It might be honor
For you, but for me it's disgrace.   4150
If you know enough of honor,
Young as you are, you'll see
That withstanding two assaults
From me is a genuine prize.
I have no desire to go on   4155

Fighting this fight: let's settle
Our quarrel and be done." "Duke,"
Said Cligès, "that's not enough.
You need to say these things
Out loud, so no one thinks   4160
You've done me a favor or granted
Me your mercy. If you wish us
To be at peace, you must
Admit it openly, in the presence
Of all who've assembled here."   4165
The duke made his words public,
And thus they arranged their peace—
But however arranged, their treaty
Brought honor only to Cligès.
And the Greeks roared with approval,   4170
But the Saxons could barely smile:
They'd seen how clearly their lord
Was weakening, tired and defeated;
They knew he'd never have offered
Such a settlement, if a better   4175
Could have been won. He'd gladly
Have ripped the heart from Cligès's
Body, if he could. So the duke
Returned to his Saxon home,
Sorrowful, sad, and shamed,   4180
Knowing none of his men
Could think him much of a man,
But defeated, and weak, and afraid.
The Saxon armies went home,
Covered with shame, and the Greeks   4185
Could see no reason for lingering;
They headed for Constantinople,

Rejoicing and happy. Truly,
The road had been opened before them
By Cligès's courage and skill.   4190
But the emperor of Germany no longer
Needed to escort them; he said
Farewell to his daughter, to Cligès,
And, last of all, to Emperor
Alis, then stayed at home.   4195
And the Greek emperor went on
His way, wonderfully happy.
And Cligès, wise and well-bred,
Recalling his father's final
Words, decided to seek   4200
His uncle's permission to leave
Constantinople and Alis's
Court and travel to Britain,
For he longed to visit Gawain,
His uncle, and see, and speak with,   4205
And come to know King Arthur.
Presenting himself before
The emperor, he asked for leave
To go to England, there
To visit his uncle and his friends.   4210
He made this request carefully,
In proper form, but Alis
Denied it, listening to all
His nephew said, but answering:
"My dear, dear nephew, I can't   4215
Agree to let you go.
It's out of the question. Saying
Farewell to you would be far
Too painful, for my heart's desire

Is to have you sit beside me   4220
And share the rule of this empire."
But Cligès was neither pleased
Nor impressed, hearing his uncle
Refuse to allow him leave.
"My lord," he said, "it would not   4225
Be proper for someone so young
And untried and knowing so little
As myself to sit at your side
And share the rule of this empire.
Gold must be put to the test   4230
Before we can tell how good
It is. I need to be tested,
Too, to be sure of my worth.
I wish to test and prove
Myself in what seems to me   4235
The best place for such trials:
Britain, where I know I can learn
If I'm truly brave, for there
I can test my strength and courage
In the company of many men   4240
Of immense honor and fame,
For whoever yearns for fame
And honor must seek it in such
A company, where the things he seeks
Are there to be found. I've sought   4245
Your permission to go there, but you need
To know, without any doubt,
That whether you send me or not,
Whether you say I can go
Or don't, I am going to Britain."   4250
"Dear nephew, I'd rather give you

Leave to go, seeing
That neither my orders nor wishes
Are able to keep you here.
May God make you willing   4255
And able to return to us soon!
And since neither wishes nor commands
Can keep you from going, let me
Give you a basket of gold
And a basket of silver, and whatever   4260
Horses you want from my stable,
All for your pleasure." He'd hardly
Finished speaking when Cligès
Warmly thanked him. The emperor
Was as good as his word: whatever   4265
He'd promised his nephew was promptly
Brought and set before him.
Cligès would travel with all
The companions he wanted, and anything
Else; for himself he had chosen   4270
Four fine horses of different
Coats, one sorrel, one tawny,
One white, one black.
                        I've forgotten
Something I should never forget:
Cligès had gone to say   4275
Farewell to Fenice, his beloved,
Intending to commend her to God.
But as soon as he saw her, he fell
To his knees and began to weep
So freely that his tears wet   4280
His tunic with its ermine trim,
And he stared at the ground, unable

To face her directly—almost
As if he'd done her some wrong,
Something that made him ashamed: 4285
He looked like a guilty man.
And Fenice, a poor, innocent
Girl, watched him, unable
To understand what was happening.
She found it hard to speak: 4290
"My friend—my brother—rise!
Sit down—right here—don't cry,
Tell me what it is you want."
"Lady, how can I speak?
Or be silent? I ask for your leave."   4295
"For what?" "I'm going to Britain."
"But tell me why, before
I grant you permission to go."
"Lady, as he lay near death,
My father begged me not   4300
To allow anything to keep me
From going to Britain, where I'd find
A host of worthy knights.
Nothing in all the world
Could make me disregard   4305
His advice. To travel from here
To Britain will not be wearisome.
The road from Greece is too long;
If I went through Greece I'd find
The trip from Constantinople   4310
To Britain far too long.
I'd be wrong to go without
Asking your leave, for I'm yours
To command." What sobs and sighs

Were concealed and restrained, as they parted!   4315
Anyone whose eyes were open
Could have seen, clearly and without
Any doubt, the simple truth
That these two loved one another.
Granted his leave, Cligès   4320
Had gone, despite how it hurt;
He was lost in his thoughts, as he went,
As the emperor was, and many
Others; but Fenice was the worst,
Finding no bottom, no shore,   4325
To the flood of thoughts that filled her,
Forever rising in her mind.
She was lost in her thoughts, still,
When she traveled to Greece with the emperor,
Welcomed and received and honored   4330
As empress and queen: her heart
And her hopes had gone with Cligès,
Wherever he was, and only
He could bring her back
Her heart, he too fatally   4335
Stricken with love. They could only
Be cured together, and whatever
It would cost one, it would cost
The other. The price she was paying
Could be read in her pallid face.   4340
Her complexion faded, lost
The clear fresh color Nature
Had put on her cheeks. She wept
Often, and she sighed often:
What could the whole empire   4345
Offer, with all its honors,

Now that Cligès was gone?
She kept rehearsing in her heart
Those moments when he'd said farewell,
How his color changed, and went pale,   4350
His tears and his sorrowful face,
How he'd come before her, weeping,
And humbly fallen to his knees,
As if in adoration.
How sweet and pleasant it was,   4355
Remembering, reminding herself!
And then, to freshen the taste
In her mouth, she dropped a bit
Of spice on her tongue, words
She'd give all Greece to be sure   4360
He'd meant when he said them, not
Speaking politely but in earnest,
For these were words that fed
Her soul, and she wanted no others:
These words kept her alive   4365
And eased the pain she lived with.
She needed nothing else
To drink, nothing else to eat:
For when he'd said farewell
He'd told her he was hers to command.   4370
How refreshing these few brief words!
They traveled straight from tongue
To heart; she set them in her mouth
To keep them forever safe,
Not daring to entrust this treasure   4375
To some different hiding place.
Where could she hold them half
As well as deep in her heart?

She never allowed them out,
Fearing robbers and brigands.   4380
But all her fears were for nothing:
No thieving bird would peck at
Her heart, for words don't change,
And words of love build
Such solid structures that their walls   4385
Won't fall, even in floods or fires;
No one can steal them away.
In truth, she wasn't sure
What she had; she sweated and struggled
To understand precisely   4390
The meaning she should give to these words.
She could take them different ways.
She asked herself questions, and gave herself
Answers, arguing in her mind:
"When Cligès said, 'I'm yours   4395
To command,' what could he mean
Except that Love made him speak?
How else could I command him?
Why else would he value me
So dearly as to make me his queen?   4400
He's far more beautiful than me,
And nobler—of much higher rank!
Only Love could cause him
To give me so precious a gift,
For I, being bound by Love,   4405
Know from my own experience
He'd never have spoken unless
He loved me, as I would never
Be his, or say I was,
If Love hadn't made it so.   4410

The only reason Cligès
Would say he was mine to command
Was that Love compelled him to say it.
If he didn't love me, he wouldn't
Fear me. Having given me   4415
To him, Love may give him to me.
Yet I worry, still, that choosing
Such ordinary words
May mean he was mocking me.
There are those who regularly flatter   4420
Women, even strangers:
'I, with all I own,
Am yours to command.' They lie
Like jackdaws! What should I
Believe? Perhaps he really   4425
Meant no more than flattery.
But I saw his color change,
And I saw the tears he shed.
There's nothing false or feigned,
It seems to me, in a flood   4430
Of tears, and a sorrowful face,
And a pallid complexion. I saw
Those tears fall from his eyes,
And eyes are never deceitful.
I know so little—but I saw   4435
So many signs of love!
Oh, but I'm thinking too much!
How horrible to learn and remember,
When so much that I've learned has been bad!
Bad? Yes, by God,   4440
It's killing me, not to see
This man who's stolen my heart,

Who's flattered and mocked me with his words!
His flowing phrases, and his flattery,
Have persuaded my heart to leave   4445
Its home, and it won't come back,
Not loving me any more,
But him. This man who's captured
My heart, how badly he's behaved!
He doesn't love me, I know it,   4450
Though he's taken everything I have.
If I know it, why did he weep?
Why? He needed no excuse,
He'd reason enough, and to spare.
I needn't think it was me: 4455
Taking leave of people
You know and love is always
Hard. Saying farewell
To his friends left him unhappy,
So he wept. It's not surprising!   4460
But advising him to visit
Britain was exactly like tearing
The heart right out of my breast!
That's a real loss, losing
Your heart. Some people deserve   4465
To suffer, but I don't—not at all!
Oh, but how can Cligès
Kill me and not be killed
In return? But why accuse him?
He's not to blame, there's no reason.   4470
Cligès would never have gone
So far away—he couldn't!—
If his heart had ached like mine.
It doesn't, it can't, I know it!

But my heart has been joined to his,   4475
Never to part: wherever
It goes, his heart will take mine
With it; it will follow him
Forever, it belongs to him.
But to tell the truth, his heart   4480
And mine are totally different.
What's the difference between them?
His heart is master, and mine
Is servant, and no matter what,
The servant must tend to his master   4485
And forget about himself.
And I have. But he doesn't give
A thought to me or my heart.
What an awful arrangement, making
His heart the master of mine!   4490
Why can't my heart by itself
Be the equal of his? Then
Our hearts could share their power.
But mine is a prisoner, and goes
Nowhere without his permission;   4495
Yet wherever his decides
To go, mine must follow
Along behind. Oh God,
Why can't our bodies be close
Enough so I could somehow   4500
Snatch mine back? Snatch
It back? Oh wicked fool,
If its happiness were taken
Away, it would die: it can stay
Where it is! I don't want to move it: 4505
I want it to stay with its master

Until he grants it his mercy,
As he certainly should, for there
Where it is, and has been, is a foreign
Land to my heart. If it learns   4510
To serve and flatter him well,
Like those who live at court,
It might return to me richer
Than it went. If you wish your lord
And master to seat you at his side,   4515
As favored servants do,
You must brush the feathers from his hair,
Even when there's nothing there.
But that creates a problem:
If you're always praising his words   4520
And his ways, but in fact at bottom
He's base and evil, you won't be
Honest enough to tell him.
He'll always believe that no one
And nothing can match him for wisdom   4525
And sense, bravery and truth —
For he'll always believe his flatterer.
How can he know himself,
See himself as he is?
If he's cruel, indifferent, extravagant,   4530
Wicked, timid as a rabbit,
Crazy, crippled, a miser,
Vulgar in speech and actions,
The flatterer fawns to his face,
But mocks when he turns his back,   4535
Puffs and praises, when he speaks
To others, if he knows his master's
Listening (pretending, of course,

Not to be aware of that fact),
But lets a nasty tongue   4540
Run wild, when his master can't hear.
If his master feels like lying,
The flatterer thinks that's fine,
Running off at the mouth
And swearing it's holy truth.   4545
You can't live at court,
And with lords, without telling
Lies. Must my heart tell falsehoods,
Longing for my lord's favor?
Must it fawn and flatter? But Cligès   4550
Is so good a knight, so honest,
So true, that my heart need never
Falsify a thing
To praise him, whatever it says,
For he is pure perfection.   4555
Why else would my heart want to serve him?
The peasants have a proverb:
'You have to be worse than wicked,
If a virtuous knight can't improve you.' "
        Thus Love tormented Fenice   4560
With such delightful sorrow
That she couldn't leave it alone.
Meanwhile, Cligès had crossed
The sea and come to Wallingford,
And he'd taken luxurious lodgings,   4565
Sparing no expense.
But Fenice was forever in his thoughts;
He never forgot her for a moment.
Meanwhile, secluding himself,
Cligès sent out his men,   4570

Seeking news of Arthur
And his barons. They soon reported
Back that the whole court,
Including the king, was engaged
In a great tournament, set   4575
In the fields outside of Oxford,
Not far from Wallingford.
The lists would be open and active
For a full four days. But Cligès
Could easily afford to stay   4580
Where he was and still be equipped
And ready in time: the tournament
Was not scheduled to start
For more than another two weeks.
He immediately sent three   4585
Of his men to London, directing
Them to bring him three
Completely different sets
Of armor, one black, one red,
One green. But when they returned,   4590
They'd completely cover over
Each color with brand-new linen,
So no one would know, as they carried
Weapons and armor to Oxford,
What markings the equipment bore.   4595
His squires hurried to London
And quickly found exactly
What their master wanted. No sooner
Said than done, and back
They came, as fast as they could.   4600
When Cligès was shown what they'd brought,
He was more than pleased, and praised them.

He put this new equipment
With what Alis had given him,
Near the Danube, when he'd dubbed him   4605
A knight, and had it all hidden
Away. You may want to ask me
Why he did these things,
But I've no intentions of telling,
For you'll have it all explained   4610
As soon as you're told that all
The barons on earth had mounted
Their horses, to compete for glory.
      And so, on the day appointed,
These worthy barons assembled.   4615
King Arthur had picked the best
Of his knights, and set their camp
Not far from Oxford. But most
Of the knights came riding in
From Wallingford. Don't wait   4620
For me to stop my story,
Here, and tell you "Such-
And-such a king was there,
And count, and duke, and prince."
When all the barons had gathered   4625
(As in those days they always did),
A strong and powerful knight
From King Arthur's court galloped
His horse between their ranks
As a sign that the tourney had begun.   4630
But no one came forward, dared
To challenge him in combat;
No one moved a muscle.
People began to ask,

"What are they waiting for,   4635
Those knights, that none comes forward?
Someone has got to start!"
And others said, "Don't
You see the sort of opponent
We're being asked to challenge?   4640
No matter how you measure them,
This is one of the four
Best knights in the world." "Who is it,
Then?" "Can't you see?
It's Sagremor the Wild!"   4645
"It is?" "Without any doubt."
Mounted on his horse, Morel,
Wearing armor blacker
Than a ripe blackberry, Cligès
Listened to the knights talking,   4650
Then spurred Morel forward,
Out of the ranks. And everyone
Turned this way and that,
Quickly asking his neighbor,
"He holds his lance like a very   4655
Practiced knight. All
His weapons and armor look good.
His shield is beautifully hung
From his neck. But he must be a fool
To accept a challenge like this,   4660
Facing one of the very
Best knights anyone knows of!
Where is he from? What country?
Who knows him?" "Not me!" "Me neither!
There's not much snow on his armor!"   4665
"That armor's blacker than a monk's

Mantle!" "Or a priest's, by God!"
    The two combatants heard
This talk, but spurred their horses
Quickly forward, both of them   4670
Eager, anxious to begin
The fighting. Cligès struck
So hard that he pinned his opponent's
Arm to his shield, his shield
To his body, and Sagremor fell.   4675
Cligès was well within
His rights to claim him as a captive,
And Sagremor yielded at once.
          And now the battle began,
There was fighting all over the field.   4680
Cligès swung into combat,
Hunting opponents wherever
He found them, defeating every
Knight he encountered. Up
And down the field he rode,   4685
And everywhere he went
The knights he fought were out
Of the tourney. Combat with Cligès
Became a test of courage;
Fighting with him was better   4690
Than capturing anyone else.
Even the prisoners he took
Shared in his glory, for at least
They had dared oppose him. No one
Could disagree: Cligès   4695
Was awarded tournament honors.
      Fighting done for the day,
He abandoned the field and went quietly

Back to his lodgings, so no one
Could ask him anything. And to keep   4700
People from seeking out
The knight in black armor, which he'd been,
He locked that suit of armor
In a room, where no one would find it,
And hung his green armor   4705
Out on the street, where all
Who looked could see it. Anyone
Hunting the knight in black
Would hunt in vain: that knight
Had left no visible traces,   4710
But completely vanished from sight.
        And thus he stayed in the city,
Disguised and hidden away,
And the knights he'd taken prisoner
Went wandering up and down,   4715
Seeking their invisible captor.
No one knew where to send them.
Even King Arthur, anxious
To greet him, had no idea
Where to look. "No one's seen him,"   4720
He was told, "since the combat was over.
No one knows where he's gone."
The king sent twenty servants,
And more, to hunt him out,
But Cligès had hidden himself   4725
So well that they found not a trace.
King Arthur crossed himself
When they told him how no one, noble
Or peasant, had the slightest notion
Where they might find him; they could   4730

Have looked in Caesarea,*
Or Iraklion,** or Toledo.
"By my faith," said the king, "I don't
Understand, but it's quite remarkable.
Perhaps he's a ghost or a phantom   4735
That's come among us. He defeated
A host of knights, and some
Of the best in the world became
His prisoners, but where do we find him?
Where is he from? How   4740
Can his captives honor their pledge?"
The king was speaking his mind,
Though he might have done better to be quiet.
The knight in black was all
The barons could talk of, that night;   4745
No one else was of interest.
          The next day, they took up arms
Again, no better informed
Than before. And Lancelot
Of the Lake came riding out first—   4750
No one could call him a coward.
He rode through the ranks, in challenge,
And Cligès came to meet him,
Green as the grass in the field,
On a horse with a tawny mane.   4755
And as he rode out, no one,
Long-haired or bald, could keep
From staring; all up and down
They were saying, "This one seems,

*Coastal crusader city then in Palestine, now in Israel.
**In Crete.

By God, a better knight,   4760
And even nobler than the black one
Who beat us so badly before,
As the pine tree's better than the elm,
Or the laurel than the elderberry.
We still don't know who the other one   4765
Was, but this one, today,
Will have to give us his name!
Who knows what this knight is called?"
But no one could say, for no one
Had ever seen him before.   4770
His beauty outshone the black knight,
And even outshone Lancelot.
Had this one been dressed in a sack,
And Lancelot all in silver,
The unknown knight would look better!   4775
As they both spurred their horses
And came dashing together, he became
The instant favorite. Cligès
Struck so fierce a blow
Straight at the lion on Lancelot's   4780
Shield that he threw him out
Of his saddle, and made him his prisoner.
Like it or not, Lancelot
Was unable to defend himself.
And then the fighting began,   4785
And the smashing and clattering of lances.
Those who fought on Cligès's
Side were full of confidence,
Knowing that everyone he fought
Would inevitably fall before him,   4790
Driven from their horses to the dust.

Cligès's successes, that day,
Were so enormous that the knights
On his side were delighted, for they doubled
The honors, and the prisoners, they'd taken   4795
The day before. But as darkness
Fell, Cligès hurried
Back to his lodgings, as fast
As he could, and hung the bright red
Armor outside his door.   4800
The armor he'd been wearing that day
Was once again locked
Away, hidden from sight.
And again the knights he'd captured
Hunted up and down,   4805
And in vain; no one could find him.
Most of the talk, that night,
Was of him, and was nothing but praise.
          Rested and fresh, the next day
Knights took up their arms.   4810
And a knight of great fame joined
The ranks at Oxford; his name
Was Perceval of Wales.
As soon as Cligès saw him
And heard his name, and knew   4815
Who he was, the longing to meet him
In combat rose in his heart.
He galloped out of the ranks
On a Spanish horse, wearing
Bright red armor. Everyone   4820
Watching gaped in astonishment,
All of them saying at once
They had never seen so dashing,

So handsome a knight. The two
Champions pursued the challenge   4825
At once, neither wanting
To wait. They spurred their horses,
And spears struck such violent
Blows on shields that, short
And stout as their lances were,   4830
They arched and bent. And then,
With everyone watching, Cligès
Smashed him out of the saddle
And with as few words as possible
Made Perceval his prisoner.   4835
And with Perceval out of action
The day's combat began,
Ranging across the field.
Every knight that Cligès
Attacked was driven to the ground.   4840
He was never out of the fighting,
Not for even an hour.
And throughout the tourney he fought
Like a moving tower of stone,
But never fighting more than one   4845
At a time, which the rules forbade,
In those days. His shield was an anvil
On which all his opponents hammered,
Smashing it to little pieces,
But none struck it without   4850
Being hit and driven from their horses,
As all day long, they were all
Agreed, the knight in red
Was never conquered; when darkness
Came, he was still the champion.   4855

And the best and wisest wished
To make his acquaintance, when the fighting
Was done, but no one could do it,
For as soon as the sun went down
He hid himself away.   4860
And he hid his bright red shield
And all the rest of his armor,
And displayed in front of his lodgings,
Instead, the very different
Arms and armor Alis   4865
Had conferred on him, in making
Him a knight. And those
He'd beaten in combat, now
Aware that a single knight
Had defeated them all, couldn't find him,   4870
For every day he'd changed
His horse and armor, each day
Seeming to be someone else.
My lord Gawain swore
He'd never seen such a knight,   4875
And declared he so wished to make
His acquaintance and know his name
That, to open the next day's tourney,
He'd throw down the challenge himself.
He was careful not to boast,   4880
Though it just might be, he thought,
That despite the havoc wrought
With a lance, the stranger's every
Encounter ending in glory,
Swordplay might be different,   4885
For Gawain knew no equal
With a blade. Tomorrow he meant

Who entered; they washed, and were seated.
Then the king took Cligès by the hand
And seated him where Arthur could see
And speak to him, for he longed to learn
As much of the stranger as he could.   5020
Why tell you what food they ate?
Meat was piled as high
On their plates as if cows could be bought
For a penny! And when all had eaten,
The king began to speak: 5025
"My friend," he said, "tell me,
Please, if pride kept you
Away from my court when you came
To this country? Why have you stayed
A stranger to us? Why did you   5030
Change the color of your arms
Every day? Tell me your name,
If you please, and where you're from."
Cligès replied, "I'll tell you
Everything." He proceeded to answer   5035
Every question the king
Had asked. And knowing who he was,
The king embraced him, joyously.
The whole court was delighted,
But none more than Gawain,   5040
Who was happiest of all to greet him.
They all took him in their arms,
And all the talk, that day,
Was about his beauty and courage.
And the king honored him more   5045
Than any of his nephews.
                    Cligès

Remained with the king until
The bright days of summer
Returned, accompanying Arthur
Through Britain, Normandy,   5050
And France, performing deeds
Of chivalry and proving his valor.
          But the love consuming his heart
Burned with no less heat,
And day after day he longed   5055
For the same distant face.
And even as he thought of Fenice,
His heart tortured him for her.
So he took his leave, and left:
He had been too long denied   5060
A glimpse of her for whom
He thirsted as for no one else,
And could no longer do without.
He said his farewells, made ready,
And traveled back to Greece.   5065
King Arthur and my lord Gawain
Were deeply sorrowful, I believe,
Finding they could not keep him.
But Cligès had already taken
Too long to return to Fenice: 5070
He hurried over land
And sea, but to him it seemed slow,
So great was his longing to see
The one who had captured his heart.
She'd paid him a proper ransom,   5075
Giving as good as she'd gotten,
For her heart had gone to him;
Her love was as great as his.

Hearts had been exchanged,
But no words, no pledges, and Cligès   5080
Was unsure, and angry at himself,
As Fenice was full of reproaches
For herself, half dead with love,
Unable to enjoy whatever
She saw, or find any pleasure,   5085
Since the things she saw were not him.
For all she knew, he was dead;
Her heart suffered in torment.
Yet every day he came closer,
Blown by a blessed wind,   5090
Untroubled by storms, until
At last, his heart joyful,
He arrived in Constantinople.
        When the city heard the news
The emperor was delighted, but who   5095
Could possibly doubt that the empress
Was a hundred times as happy?
Cligès and all his men
Had returned straight to Greece.
The noblest and greatest barons   5100
Came to the port to greet him,
But the emperor preceded them all,
With the empress at his side—and seeing
Cligès, Alis ran
And right in front of the world   5105
Embraced him. Greeting each other,
Fenice and Cligès blushed
But somehow miraculously managed,
Finding themselves standing
So close, not to fall   5110

Straight into each other's
Arms, hugging and kissing
As Love would have liked. But what folly
That would have been! People
Came running to see him, and all   5115
Rejoiced at his coming: they led him
To the heart of the city, the royal
Palace, in a great procession,
Some mounted, some on foot.
The celebration needs   5120
No description—the words that were spoken,
The honor and respect shown him,
The entire city, one
And all, doing their best
To delight Cligès with their welcome.   5125
        His uncle gave Cligès
Everything he had, except
His crown; to keep his nephew
Happy, he told him to take
Whatever he wanted from the imperial   5130
Treasury. But money was not
On Cligès's mind: he dreamed of,
But did not dare to speak to,
Fenice; he longed to speak,
But was afraid. He saw her every   5135
Day, he sat close by her,
Alone; there was nothing to stop him,
No one made objections.
        He'd been home a very long time.
One day he came to her room,   5140
She who was hardly his enemy,
And no one should be surprised

That her door was not shut
In his face. He sat close by her,
And stayed long after everyone   5145
Else had gone, so no one
Was there to see or hear
Or stop him from speaking. Fenice
Had been asking him questions about Britain,
And then she'd turned to the subject   5150
Of my lord Gawain and what
He was like; and finally she reached
A matter closer to her heart
And her fears. She asked him if,
In Britain, there'd been anybody   5155
He might have fallen in love with.
Cligès answered at once,
Having no reason to delay;
She'd asked him a simple question,
And he answered, "My lady, I loved   5160
In Britain, but no one who was there.
Like a tree stripped of its bark,
My heart had gone out of its body.
The very day I left
Germany, my heart left me.   5165
But where did it go? Here,
I think. My heart was here,
My body was there. And now
That I'm back, I cannot leave,
For here is where my heart is;   5170
I followed my heart here.
But it won't return to my body,
Nothing I do can compel it,
And I would not wish it if there were.

But you—how have you been,   5175
Since you came to Constantinople?
Have you been happy here?
Do you like the country? The people?
How can I ask you anything
More? Do you like the country?"   5180
"I haven't liked it, till now,
But now, for some reason, I do.
And this is a pleasure, my friend,
I hope I never lose,
For my heart will never give it   5185
Up, and I'll never force it.
All I have left is the bark,
For I live with no heart: it's gone.
I've never been to Britain,
But my heart has gone there without me   5190
And made its own arrangements."
"Lady, when was it there?
Tell me when it went,
What season, and exactly when:
If this is something I   5195
Should hear, and no one else,
Tell me. When I was there?"
"Yes, but you didn't know.
It was there when you were there,
And it left Britain when you did."   5200
"My God, I neither knew
Nor saw. Why not, my lady?
If only I'd known—oh,
What a wonderful companion I'd have had!"
"And I would have known such comfort!   5205
I know you'd have treated it well—

As I would have treated yours,
If you'd left it here or let
Me know where it was." "My lady,
Of course it came to you!"   5210
"To me? Then it wasn't in exile
At all, for mine was with you."
"Lady, you must have had
A pair of hearts, for mine,
I tell you, belongs to you."   5215
"My friend, you've taken mine,
And so we're in full agreement!
You must know, as God is my witness,
Your uncle's had nothing of me:
It was not what I wanted, and he had   5220
No chance. He's never known me
In the way that Adam knew Eve.
They call me 'my lady,' but they're wrong:
Those who call me a lady
Don't know I'm still a girl.   5225
Even your uncle doesn't know,
For he's drunk a magic potion
And thinks he's awake, when he's sleeping:
He thinks he's had his pleasure
Of me, he thinks he lies   5230
In my arms, but let me assure you,
I lie elsewhere in our bed.
My heart and my body are yours,
And no one can think there's anything
Wrong with that gift, for the moment   5235
My heart was given to you
My body was part of that promise,
And no one else must have it.

I never expected to be cured
Of the wound Love gave me, for you,   5240
But however much I've suffered
For loving you, and being
Loved, no one can call you
Tristan or me Iseult:
Love is not worthy of its name   5245
When it's wrong, and people can say so.
Whatever pleasure you can take
In my body, now, is all
You can have, unless you can find
A way to separate me   5250
From your uncle, to take me somewhere
Where he can never find me,
Nor accuse either of us,
Nor know whom to blame.
Think about this, tonight,   5255
And tomorrow tell me whatever
Solution you can find—as I
Will try to do. Come
To my rooms tomorrow, come
In the morning and we'll talk, we'll tell   5260
Each other whatever we've thought;
And then we'll decide, as best
We can, the best thing to do."
          Hearing what Fenice wanted,
Cligès swore his agreement;   5265
Her plan was a good one. He was joyful
As he left, and so he remained.
All that night they lay
In their beds, happily wakeful,
Turning over and over   5270

In their minds the things they might do.
They met, the next day, as early
As they could, and discussed, in private,
The plans they each had formed.
Cligès was the first to speak,   5275
And told her his nighttime thoughts:
"My lady," he said, "I can't
Believe there's a better solution
Than exile in Britain, the place
Where I can best bring you: 5280
Don't say you won't go: please!
When Paris brought beautiful
Helen to Troy, her welcome
Was joyous, but not so splendid
As yours and mine will be,   5285
All through the lands ruled
By King Arthur, my uncle. But if
Britain is not acceptable,
Tell me what you prefer,
For I'm ready to do as you wish,   5290
No matter what happens." Fenice
Answered, "I'll tell you. I can't
Run away like that:
They'd talk about us, all
Across the world, as if   5295
We were Tristan and Iseult. The moment
We fled, no matter where
We went, everyone here
And there would accuse us of wild
Passion. No one would care   5300
That it wasn't true. Who
Would believe that, somehow or other,

I managed to escape from your uncle
Still a virgin? They'd call me
A shameless whore, and you   5305
They'd call a fool. It's better
To remember Saint Paul's advice,
And follow it: he teaches that those
Who can't remain chaste should always
Carefully arrange their affairs   5310
So no one knows what they're doing
And no one can criticize.
Slanderous tongues should be silenced—
And unless you object, I know
Exactly how to do it.   5315
Let them think I died:
That's my plan. I'll pretend
To be sick, I'll stay in my bed,
And you, in the meantime, will have
A tomb erected, making   5320
Sure that both my coffin
And the tomb are so constructed
That I can lie in them safely
And breathe, and stay alive,
Without arousing suspicion.   5325
Build it somewhere where you
Can come in the darkness and take me
Out, and no one will see.
And no one but you should bring me
Whatever I'll need—you,   5330
To whom I'll belong completely.
For the rest of my life I wish
To serve no one but you.
You'll be my master and my servant;

I'll love you, whatever you do,   5335
And I'll never be queen of an empire
Unless you're its emperor. If you
And I are together, no place,
No matter how dim and dark,
Could help but be brighter than a palace.   5340
Being with you, having
You, and seeing you,
Will make me queen of the world
And all the treasure in it.
And if this is done as it should be,   5345
No one will ever reproach us,
For no one will know what was done:
Everyone in all the empire
Will believe me buried in the earth.
And Thessala, my governess and nurse,   5350
In whom I trust, will help me,
For she's wise, and I'll put myself
In her hands." Having heard her words,
He replied, "Lady, if this
Can be done, and you're sure Thessala   5355
Can tell you how, there's nothing
Left but to make ourselves ready
And act as quickly as we can.
But the thing must be done wisely:
If we fail, everything's lost.   5360
There's a master builder I'll talk to,
A man who can carve anything;
He's known all over the world
For the things he's built, for the portraits
He's painted, for the sculptures he's carved.   5365
His name is John, and he's mine.

There isn't a craft in the world,
No matter what, he can't
Master, if he tries, for compared
To him all the others   5370
Are beginners, mere babes at the breast.
Craftsmen from Antioch
And Rome have learned their arts
By imitating him.
And there's no one more loyal. I'll sound   5375
Him out, and if I find
He'll do what I want, and be quiet,
I'll set him free, he
And his heirs. I'll tell him no lies,
But exactly what we're doing,   5380
If he solemnly swears he'll help
In good faith and never breathe
A word to anyone."
She answered, "Let it be done!"
       So Cligès took his leave   5385
And left her. And Fenice sent
For Thessala, whom she'd brought
To Constantinople with her,
Taking her away from her native
Country. The governess came   5390
At once, without delay,
But had no idea what was wanted.
She asked Fenice, in private,
To tell her why she'd been summoned.
And the empress hid nothing,   5395
But told her every detail:
"Nurse," she said, "I know
No one else will hear

Whatever I tell you, for they never
Have: you've always proved   5400
Yourself the wisest of the wise.
And I love you for all you've done.
I've always told you my problems,
And I've sought no other help.
You know why I lie awake,   5405
And who I think of, and want.
My eyes see nothing they like,
Except one thing, which I'm not
Permitted to enjoy, except
At a terrible cost. But I've found   5410
My match, my mate: if I long
For him, he longs for me,
And if I'm in pain he suffers
From my sorrow, he feels my sadness.
And now, let me tell you   5415
What I've been thinking and saying,
And what the two of us
Have agreed to do." And then
She explained her plan, how
She meant to pretend illness   5420
And suffering, and so much pain
And weakness she would seem to die,
And Cligès would come at night
And take her, "And I'll live with him
Forever!" She could not live   5425
For long, in any other way.
But with Thessala's help
She was sure it could all be managed,
And everything she wanted
And longed for would come to pass.   5430

"And yet my joy arrives
So slowly, and comes from so far!"
The governess promised to help her
In every possible way.
There was nothing to fear, for she   5435
Would arrange it so carefully and well,
Now that she knew what was wanted,
That no one who saw her mistress
Could possibly think her soul
Had not flown from her body;   5440
She'd mix Fenice such a potion
That her whole body would grow cold
And lose its color, turn pale,
She'd forget how to speak and breathe,
And yet still be healthy   5445
And alive, but feeling no pain,
Aware in her coffin and tomb
Neither of pleasure nor grief
For one whole day and night.
       Fenice had listened carefully,   5450
And when Thessala had done, she said,
"Nurse. It's all in your hands.
There's nothing more I need do.
I'm yours. Take good care.
Now tell the visitors here   5455
I'm able to see no one.
I'm sick, and there's too much noise."
Thessala made the announcement.
"Gentlemen: my mistress is ill
And wishes you to leave,   5460
For there's too much talking and noise,
And it's making her illness worse.

She won't be able to rest
In peace until you leave her.
As far as I can recall,   5465
I've never heard her complain
Like this, so I'm deeply concerned.
Leave her, but don't be angry:
She'll speak to no one, tonight."
They left, as she requested.   5470
And Cligès sent for John,
Who came to his lodgings in secret,
And said to his servant, "John,
Do you know what I want to tell you?
Your life is mine, you belong   5475
To me, I can sell you or give you
Away, body and soul
And belongings, like anything else
I own. But I can tell you,
If you like, a plan I have   5480
That would set you free forever,
You and all of your heirs."
And John, who desperately longed
For freedom, answered at once:
"My lord," he said, "I'm ready   5485
To do whatever you ask,
If it means my freedom, and freedom
For my wife and children. Tell me
What needs to be done! You couldn't
Command a task too troublesome,   5490
Too hard, or long, or painful;
Nothing will be too much.
And even if it works against me,
I'll do it, and gladly, and forget

My own concerns." "It's true,   5495
John: this is something
I can't so much as speak of
Unless you swear the most solemn
Oath, the most sacred vow,
To serve me with absolute faith   5500
And never tell a soul."
"Gladly, my lord," said John.
"And you'd be wrong to doubt me!
I swear the most solemn oath
Never, as long as I live,   5505
To say the least little thing
That could hurt you in any way."
"John, were I burned at the stake
I wouldn't dare confess
What I need to tell you: I'd sooner   5510
They plucked out my eyes. But I trust you,
I've seen your loyalty and good sense,
So I'll tell you what's in my heart.
I think you'll do as I ask you;
You'll help, and you'll never talk."   5515
"In the name of God, sir, yes!"
So Cligès very quietly
Told him everything, and when John
Had heard what you already
Know (because I told you),   5520
He swore to Cligès he'd build
The most perfect tomb for his purpose
He could possibly make, and what's more,
He would bring his master to see
A house he'd built that no one   5525
Knew of or had ever seen,

Not even his wife, not even
His children, and Cligès could inspect it
And see if everything about it
Pleased him. Just let his master   5530
Accompany him, alone,
To the place where he did his work,
And he'd show Cligès the loveliest,
Most noble spot he'd ever
Seen! "Let's go, then," said Cligès.   5535
   Outside the city, off
To one side, John had constructed
A tower, beautifully made.
And after he'd led his master
Out there, he showed him all   5540
Around it; it was full of shining
Paintings, vividly colored.
He showed him everything—rooms,
Fireplaces, roof, and all.
Cligès examined this isolated   5545
Dwelling, where no one came
Or went; he went from room
To room, and studied it all.
The tower pleased him immensely:
He praised its beauty and construction.   5550
Surely his lady would be happy
Here as long as she lived,
And no one would know where she was.
"That's right, my lord: she'd be hidden,
Here. You're sure you've seen   5555
It all, my tower and its charms?
Ah, but there's more, much more,
That no one could find for himself.

Would you like to try? Search
As hard as you can, you'll never   5560
Uncover its secret places,
And neither will anyone else,
No matter how subtle or wise,
Unless I show them where they are.
You see? There's nothing missing,   5565
Nothing a lady might want:
All you have to do
Is bring her. It's comfortable, beautiful,
And as you'll see in a moment,
This tower extends underground,   5570
Though no one can find the entrance
Or know there's anything there.
The door is carved out of rock
And so cleverly made that no one
Can see more than mere stone."   5575
"Incredible!" exclaimed Cligès.
"Please lead, and I'll follow after.
I'm anxious to see the rest!"
So John led the way,
Holding his master by the hand,   5580
Until they came to a polished,
Solid door, brilliantly
Painted. Holding Cligès's
Right hand, John touched the wall.
"My lord," he said, "no one   5585
Would see the window and door
In this wall. Do you think you could get
This open, and walk right through,
Except by smashing the rock?"
Cligès declared he could not,   5590

And neither, he thought, could anyone
Else. John told him to watch,
And easily opened the door,
For he had designed and built it
And needed to damage nothing   5595
To make it open at his touch.
And then they both walked through,
And down a flight of stairs,
Into a vaulted room
Where John would work, all alone,   5600
When something needed to be made.
"My lord," he said, "of all
The men made by God
Only you and I have ever
Been here; you can see for yourself   5605
What a comfortable place it is!
Let it be your refuge,
And hide your beloved here.
It's a fitting place for such
A guest, with rooms and baths,   5610
And conduits for heated water,
Running under the ground.
Anyone seeking a better,
More comfortable hiding place
For his lady would have to hunt   5615
Incredibly hard and long.
Once you've lived in here
You'll see how delightful it is!"
John showed him everything, beautiful
Rooms with painted ceilings,   5620
Pointing to lovely work
His master found delightful

Indeed. Cligès examined
It all and said, "John,
My friend, you and yours   5625
Are free. I owe you everything!
I want my lady to live
Here; no one will know
But you and me—no one."
John said, "I thank you, my lord!   5630
We've been here long enough;
There's nothing more to do.
It's time we both returned."
"Well said," Cligès acknowledged.
"We'll leave." Retracing their steps,   5635
They went back to the tower and left.
Back in the city, they heard
People telling each other,
"Have you heard the astonishing news
About my lady the empress?   5640
May the Holy Spirit help
This excellent, sensible lady,
Who's been struck by a terrible sickness."
        Hearing these words, Cligès
Went hurrying straight to the palace,   5645
Where joy and pleasure had vanished,
And everyone grieved for the empress,
Who pretended to be mortally ill.
In fact, she suffered from nothing,
And felt herself in no pain,   5650
Though she'd told them all that no one
Could come to her rooms; her illness,
She said, had her in its grip,
Twisting her heart and her head.

But the emperor could come, and his nephew,   5655
For she'd never shut her door
To her lord, the emperor. But no one
Else would be admitted.
She'd put herself in terrible
Danger, all for Cligès,   5660
And it pained her when he did not come,
For he was all she wanted.
But, soon, Cligès would be there,
Telling her everything he
Had seen, all the wonders   5665
He'd found. He came, and he told her,
But he did not stay there long,
For Fenice wanted the world
To think his visit troublesome,
And called out, "Go! Leave me!   5670
I can't have you here!
I'm far too ill for visits,
And I fear I'll never be better!"
Cligès admired her acting;
He left, his face wreathed   5675
In the fiercest sorrow ever
Seen. How sad he seemed!
But his heart was jumping with joy,
For he knew what happiness was coming.
        And so, healthy as she was,   5680
The empress pretended to be sick
And suffering, but the gullible emperor's
Sadness and suffering were real.
He tried to send her doctors,
But she refused to see them,   5685
Declaring they could not touch her.

What most worried her husband
Was hearing her say that one
Doctor was all she needed,
And He could easily heal her   5690
Whenever He wanted. Whether
She lived or died, she said,
Was up to Him; she put
Her health and her life in His hands.
Everyone thought she spoke   5695
Of God—but how wrong they were,
For the one she meant was Cligès:
He was the only savior
Who could cure or kill her as he wished.
  And so the empress made sure   5700
That no doctor came near her.
In order to complete her husband's
Deception, she'd neither eat
Nor drink, so soon she was pale
And discolored. Her nurse was constantly   5705
With her—and so incredibly
Sly that she'd searched the whole city
And secretly found a woman
Mortally ill and carried
Away a pot of her urine.   5710
To make the deceit perfect,
She came to see the woman
Often, saying she hoped
To cure her fatal sickness,
Bringing with her, each time,   5715
A urinal, and taking samples,
Until she saw that doctors
And potions could clearly do nothing.

That day the woman died.
But she carried away this urine,   5720
And kept it out of sight,
Waiting for the emperor to awake.
And then she hurried to find him,
Saying, "If you'd like, my lord,
Send for your doctors, for my lady's   5725
Passed this urine, which clearly
Shows her illness. She'll let
The doctors see it, if they wish,
But not in the empress's presence."
        The doctors were sent for, and came,   5730
And saw at once that the urine
Was mordantly awful, and stank,
And all agreed that the empress
Could never recover; surely
Would die by afternoon,   5735
If indeed she lasted that long;
God would be calling her soul
To come home. They spoke to each other,
Softly. The emperor bid them
Tell him the truth. They answered   5740
That none of them saw the slightest
Chance of recovery; that day,
And soon, the empress would surely
Render up her soul.
Hearing these words, the emperor   5745
And many of those around him
Could barely keep themselves
From falling to the floor. Such cries
And laments had never been heard,
Echoing through the palace.   5750

I'll spare you their sorrowful words:
You know what Thessala was up to,
Mixing the empress's potion,
Stirring and shaking all
The secret ingredients she'd long since   5755
Gathered, knowing well
In advance the things she'd need.
And Fenice drank it, before
The middle of the afternoon,
And had scarcely swallowed it down   5760
When her eyes had trouble seeing,
And her face turned as white
As if all her blood was gone.
She couldn't have moved her hands
Or feet, had they burned her alive;   5765
She lay there, still and silent,
But hearing perfectly well
How the emperor wept and lamented,
And the mourning that filled the room.
People were crying and weeping   5770
All over the city, saying,
"Oh God, what hateful, wicked
Things all-horrible Death
Has done! So greedy, so evil,
His jealousy so sudden   5775
And swift that nothing can sate him!
What a savage, ghastly bite
You've bitten out of the world!
May God confound you, Death!
You've murdered Beauty itself!   5780
You've killed what could have been
The best, most saintly woman

God has ever fashioned.
God must be patience incarnate
To let you have such power   5785
To destroy the things He creates.
It's time He turned against you
And took away your power,
For now you've gone too far,
Your arrogant pride is too much!"   5790
And thus the people raged,
Waving their arms and beating
Their palms, while priests said prayers
For the dead good lady's soul,
On which might God have mercy.   5795
        And while they wept and cried —
At least, as the story is written —
Three wizened doctors arrived
From Salerno, where they'd lived and worked
For years. All the tears   5800
And mourning caught their eye,
And they asked for whom these tears
Were shed, these laments raised?
Who was so deeply mourned?
And people gave them this answer: 5805
"My God, gentlemen! You really
Don't know? The whole world
Would surely share our madness,
If it knew our pain, and our anger,
How badly we're hurt, what a loss   5810
We suffered, earlier today.
Lord, where have you come from,
Not to know what happened
In Constantinople just now?

All right: let us tell you,   5815
For then you'll join the mourning
And sorrow that afflict us. Haven't
You heard how Death, greedy,
Rotten with longing—Death,
Who always waits for the best—   5820
Has committed the vilest crime,
He who is always vile?
God had lit the world
With a clear and brilliant light.
But Death can't change what Death   5825
Has always been, forever
Reaching out and snatching
Away the best it can find.
And now, to prove his power,
He's taken someone better   5830
Than best, better than them all—
For had he taken the world
Itself, it could not have been worse,
If only he'd left just her
Alive, just her. But he took her—   5835
And all the beauty, grace,
And wisdom a woman can have,
The things that belong to such goodness.
He plotted her death, and stole her,
He who destroys everything   5840
Good. He took our empress.
That's what Death has done!"
"God in Heaven must hate
This city," said the doctors, "if He let us
Take so long in coming.   5845
Had we been here a day

Earlier, Death wouldn't be proud
Of snatching anyone away."
"Gentlemen, the empress would never
Have allowed you to see her, or take her   5850
Under your care. She did not
Die for lack of doctors!
My lady would let none of them
Examine her or meddle
With the course of her illness. No,   5855
No, she'd never have allowed you!"
These clever doctors remembered
Solomon's wife, who hated
Her husband so much she pretended
Death to deceive him. Had the empress   5860
Done this? Perhaps they could find
Some way to revive the woman:
No one would contradict them,
No one would dare, if they unveiled
Some scheme, some treacherous plot.   5865
They hurried to the palace, where the sounds
Of mourning crashed in people's
Ears like the thundering of Heaven.
The most learned doctor, their leader,
Walked directly to the coffin.   5870
No one told him, "Don't touch her!"
No one pushed him away.
He set his hand on her chest,
And on her side, and saw
At once that the woman was alive,   5875
There was no doubt. The emperor
Stood beside the coffin,
Wracked and torn by grief,

So the doctor shouted out loud,
"Take comfort, oh mighty Emperor!   5880
I know for a fact that this lady
Lying here is not dead:
Leave off your mourning, take heart!
And if I can't bring her to life,
Kill me, hang me from a tree!"   5885
        The weeping and mourning stopped;
The palace was suddenly silent.
Then the emperor told the doctors
To do whatever was needed:
His empire was theirs to command.   5890
If they could restore his empress
To life, he'd make them lords,
But tell him a single lie
And he'd hang them like thieves. The doctor
Replied, "Agreed, my lord!   5895
Show me no mercy if I can't
Do what I said I would do.
Now: don't ask me why,
But see that everyone leaves
These rooms. No one may stay!   5900
I need to deal with this lady's
Sickness in silence, and alone.
Only my two companions
Are allowed to remain, for they
Are doctors and men I trust.   5905
Let all the others be gone!"
Cligès, John, and Thessala
Wanted to contradict him,
But they knew that everyone else
Would know there was something wrong,   5910

If they tried to get in the way.
So they held their tongues, and said
What everyone else was saying,
And quietly left the palace.
Then the three doctors ripped   5915
Away the lady's shroud,
Not bothering with knives or scissors,
And told her, "Lady, don't
Be afraid! We won't hurt you!
You can speak to us without fear!   5920
We haven't the slightest doubt
That you're alive, in good health.
Now given this fact, let's
Be sensible. No need to panic:
If good advice is what   5925
You need, we three will surely
Do our best to assist you.
Whether it's good or bad,
You can trust us not to betray you,
And hide whatever needs hiding.   5930
No long discussion is required:
We guarantee you our full
Support, our loyal service.
You'd better not refuse it."
They thought they could force her to believe   5935
Their lies, but it didn't work.
The help they'd offered to give her
Was hardly something she wanted;
They were talking nonsense, and she knew it.
Seeing they were getting nowhere   5940
With their lying words, the three
Doctors pulled her out

Of the coffin and began to beat her,
Slapping and hitting and kicking,
But despite their stupid violence   5945
She never said a word.
They tried to make her afraid,
Threatening that if she still
Stayed silent, she'd live to regret it,
For they had some terrible tricks   5950
Up their sleeves, things more awful
Than any weak woman could stand.
"You see, we know you're alive;
You simply refuse to speak.
We know you're only pretending,   5955
Trying to deceive the emperor.
Don't be afraid of us.
If someone has done you wrong,
Tell us, before we hurt you.
Let us know what you want,   5960
Or you'll force us to terrible things,
And we're only here to help you,
Whatever it may be, believe me!"
Nothing they said would work.
So they picked up whips and began   5965
To scourge her bare back,
Raising welts all over,
Striking her tender skin
So many times that it bled.
        But no matter how they whipped her,   5970
Cutting lines in her flesh
And making the blood run
Freely from her wounds, they could not
Accomplish a thing, she never

Sighed or said a word   5975
Or moved a single muscle.
So then they said they'd need
A fire and lead, for melting
And pouring into the palms
Of her hands, to make her talk.   5980
They went and fetched what they wanted,
Lit their fire and melted
The lead. And then these evil
Scoundrels tortured the lady,
Taking the red-hot lead   5985
Straight from the fire and letting it
Run all over her hands.
But even burning through
Her hands with lead was not
Enough for these miserable, cowardly   5990
Bastards, for they swore, if she didn't
Speak at once, they'd set
Her entire body on a grill
Until she was well roasted.
She remained silent, never   5995
Protesting this destruction of her flesh.
They started to fan the fire,
Prepared to set her on the grill,
When a horde of women, more
Than a thousand, broke away   6000
From the crowd and came to the door,
And through a small crack saw
The cruel and brutal treatment
Inflicted on their lady's body,
And how it would soon suffer   6005
Martyrdom by fire and flame.

They attacked the door with hammers
And axes, and broke it down —
And what a smashing, crashing
Clamor they raised, in the process!   6010
And now they could seize the doctors
And without wasting a moment
Give them the reward they deserved.
          Women poured through the palace
Door like a charging army,   6015
And Thessala among them, wanting
Nothing more than to find
Her mistress, wherever they'd put her.
She found her lying naked
In the fire, badly hurt,   6020
And quickly put her back
In the coffin and covered her over,
While the other women were giving
The three doctors what they'd asked for,
Not waiting for the emperor to return   6025
Or any of his stewards. They threw
The doctors through the open
Windows, down to the courtyard
Below, where all three died,
Their necks broken, and their ribs,   6030
Their arms, and their legs. No woman's
Work was ever better
Done! The three doctors
Had earned the wages they'd gotten,
And the mob of women had paid them.   6035
          But Cligès was terribly worried,
Hearing the incredible pain
And anguish his belovèd had suffered:

He was almost out of his mind,
Fearing—and not without cause—   6040
That the tortures the three doctors
Had inflicted could have so badly
Hurt her she might be dead
Indeed. He was overwhelmed
With despair. But Thessala brought   6045
A wonderfully precious ointment
And very gently applied it
To Fenice's ghastly wounds.
And then, for this new entombment,
The women wrapped the body   6050
In white Syrian linen,
But left the face uncovered,
Mourning the whole time,
Weeping as though it would never
End. The whole city   6055
Mourned, rich and poor
Alike, low and high,
Almost as if competing
In sorrow, not wanting to stop.
It lasted all night long.   6060
The next day Emperor Alis
Summoned John to court,
And gave him these orders: "John,
Whatever wonderful work
You've done, I want all   6065
Your skill, all your art,
To go into making a tomb
Of perfect, incomparable beauty."
Since John had already built it,
He said that he had one ready,   6070

Dazzlingly lovely and fine.
He'd always meant it to hold
The remains of some holy saint;
He'd begun the work with that plan:
"But if we honored the empress   6075
By placing her body there,
Surely it would hold a saint."
"Well said," the emperor replied.
"We'll bury her body with those
Of the other saints, in front of   6080
Saint Peter's holy cathedral.
Before she died, she begged
To be laid to eternal rest
In that sacred spot. Set
Yourself to work! And let   6085
The tomb be placed, as in justice
And law it should, on the graveyard's
Finest, most beautiful site."
John answered, "Gladly, my lord."
A past master of his art,   6090
He went to his workshop and took up
His tools. And because the stone
He built with was hard, and extremely
Cold, he set a feather
Mattress inside. To perfume   6095
The air she breathed, he put in
Fragrant flowers and leaves—
Which were wonderfully useful, concealing
From sight the soft cushioning
Lying underneath. The churches   6100
And parishes for miles around
Had finished funeral services,

And the bells were tolling, as they do
In honor of the dead. Then the body
Was lifted, and brought to the tomb,   6105
Where John had worked long and hard
To make everything splendid and fine.
And the body was set inside.
Rich and poor, everyone
In all of Constantinople   6110
Followed the body, weeping
And hurling curses at Death.
Boys and knights alike
Fainted, as did ladies and girls,
Beating their breasts and quarreling   6115
With the power that had stolen their empress:
"Oh Death," they said, "couldn't you
Have taken a ransom for our lady?
Whatever you've won, in robbing
Us, is nothing to our loss!"   6120
But Cligès's weeping and mourning
Were the most intense; staggering
Half distraught behind
The body, he came close to dying,
But kept himself alive,   6125
Waiting for the moment when he'd lift
Fenice from her tomb and learn
Whether she was alive or dead.
The emperor's barons, who would place
The body in its grave, stood waiting,   6130
But they left it to John to seal
The tomb, and turned away
Their eyes, half overcome.
And John quietly did

What he had to do; without   6135
Any help, free to work
As he chose. He sealed the tomb,
Closed it tight and bolted it
Down: no one could ever
Open anything John   6140
Had closed, unless they pried it
Up, broke it open,
Smashed the bolts and seals.
　　　And there Fenice lay,
Till the darkness fell, guarded   6145
By thirty knights with ten
Flaring torches that cast
A great clear light all around.
Exhausted by hours of mourning,
The knights' eyes were heavy.   6150
During the night they'd eaten
And drunk; soon they were all
Asleep. As darkness fell,
Cligès left the emperor's
Court, and disappeared;   6155
No knight or page or servant
Had any idea where he was.
It didn't take long for John
To join him. He gave Cligès
His best advice, and weapons   6160
(Which he would not need), then they hurried
To the tomb, spurring their horses.
A high wall enclosed
The entire graveyard, and the gates
Were shut; the sleepy knights   6165
Guarding the tomb had locked

Themselves inside, to keep
Anyone else from entering.
Cligès could not get in:
The gates were strong, the walls   6170
Were high. But he had to enter.
Love gave him the strength.
Brave and quick, he threw
Himself at the wall, and climbed it.
On the other side was an orchard,   6175
Planted thick with trees
Growing so close to the wall
They almost touched it. Their help
Was exactly what Cligès wanted:
He descended from a tree to the ground.   6180
The first thing he did was go
To the gate, and open it for John.
Seeing the knights asleep,
He extinguished all the torches,
Restoring the night's darkness.   6185
Then John unsealed the tomb
And opened it, breaking nothing
And leaving no marks. Cligès
Descended into the tomb
And carried his beloved out.   6190
She was limp and already half-dead,
He held her tight, and kissed her,
Not certain whether to weep
Or rejoice. She neither moved
Nor spoke. As quickly as he could,   6195
John resealed the tomb, leaving
No traces: everything looked
Just as it had before.

And then they hurried to the tower,
As fast as they could. As soon   6200
As they had her in the tower, and safely
Installed in the underground rooms,
They unwrapped the shroud from her body.
But Cligès had not known
Of the sleeping potion she'd drunk,   6205
Which turned her body as still
And unmoving as a corpse. No wonder
He thought she was dead! He felt
An immense despair, and began
To sigh and weep and sob.   6210
But slowly, bit by bit,
The potion lost its power.
And Fenice, who could hear but not help
Her beloved, struggled to offer
Some comfort, a word or a look;   6215
Her heart almost stopped
With the pain she felt for Cligès.
"Death!" he was crying, "What a monster
You are, sparing, ignoring
So many vile, unworthy   6220
Souls, letting them live
But taking Fenice! You drunken,
Crazy fool, killing
My beloved before you kill me!
I see an incredible sight—   6225
My beloved, dead, while I'm
Alive. Oh my love, my love!
How can I be alive
When you're dead? How right they would be
To accuse me of having killed you,   6230

Since you died on my account!
So I myself am your Death,
Beloved. Can that be right?
You've gone to your grave with my life,
And I've kept yours. But oh,   6235
My sweet! Where could my happiness
Come from, if not from your life,
As yours came from mine?
I loved no one but you:
We were two, but in truth just one.   6240
And what I've done I should never
Do, for you live in me
And I'm no longer in you,
And we should each of us always
Carry the other inside us,   6245
And nothing should keep us apart."
At these words she managed
A feeble sigh, and whispered,
"Beloved, beloved, I may be
Almost dead, but not quite.   6250
It makes no difference to me.
I thought I'd trick them all,
But now I'm truly sorry,
For Death doesn't play games.
I can't believe I'm still   6255
Alive: those doctors hurt me,
They beat me and tore at my flesh.
And yet, if my nurse could be with me,
If somehow she could come,
She could bring me back   6260
To life, if anyone can."
"Don't worry, my love," said Cligès,

"I'll see that she comes at once—
I'll have her here tonight!"
"Beloved, let John fetch her."   6265
John went. It wasn't easy
To find her, but he managed. He told her
He wanted her to come
With him, without fail and at once,
For Fenice and Cligès had sent him   6270
To find her. They were waiting in the tower,
And Fenice had been badly hurt;
She should bring along her ointments
And potions and other medicines,
For Fenice needed her help   6275
At once, and would die if she waited.
Quickly Thessala gathered
All the medicines she could,
Ointments and herbs and potions,
And hurried off with John.   6280
They left the city in secret
And headed straight for the tower.
And, seeing her nurse, Fenice
Believed herself as good
As cured, so deep was her love   6285
And trust. Cligès hugged
And kissed her: "Welcome, welcome,
Thessala! Oh how I love you!
But tell me what you think
Of this lady's wounds? How   6290
Does she seem? Do you think she'll recover?"
"Of course, my lord! No doubt
About it; I'll cure her completely!
Two weeks, or less, and she'll be

As healthy and strong as she's ever   6295
Been—and even better
Than ever!" The cure began
At once; John made sure
The tower was supplied with everything
Needed. Cligès rode boldly   6300
Back and forth, from city
To tower, without concealment,
Saying he had a hawk
Molting, and went to see it,
And no one imagined any   6305
Other reason for his constant
Visits: the hawk was good enough
Cause. Night and day
He was there, and John guarded
The tower, so no one could enter.   6310
Fenice suffered no ill
Effects: Thessala had completely
Cured her. And had he been made
Duke of Almería,
Or Morocco, or Tudela, Cligès   6315
Could not have been happier than he was.
Love had committed no crime,
Joining these two together,
For when they lay in each other's
Arms, hugging and kissing,   6320
Their joy, their pleasure, seemed
To make the world a better
Place. Can one ask for more?
There was nothing either wanted
That the other did not want: 6325
Their love and desire were shared

As if they were one and the same.
    All that year, I believe,
And a full three months of the next,
Fenice remained in the tower.   6330
But when summer returned, and leaves
Appeared on the trees, and flowers
Bloomed, and birds rejoiced,
Singing songs in their own
Language, it happened, one morning,   6335
That a nightingale sang near her window.
Cligès was embracing her sweetly,
One arm round her side, the other
Round her neck, as she held him,
And she said, "My dear good love,   6340
How nice it would be, how delightful,
To spend some time in an orchard.
I haven't seen the sun
Or the moon in fifteen months.
I'd dearly love, if I could,   6345
To be out in the light of day;
I've been locked up so long in this tower.
If there happens to be an orchard
Nearby, where I might amuse
Myself, it would do me good."   6350
Cligès promised to consult
With John, the moment he came,
And tell him what she wanted, and see
If anything might be done.
John arrived almost   6355
At once, for he came there often.
And as soon as Cligès told him
What Fenice would like, he said,

"She has an orchard at her
Command, ready and waiting.   6360
I've provided this tower with everything
Your lady could possibly want."
Fenice was overjoyed
And asked John to be brought there.
"No reason why not," he said.   6365
Then John opened a secret
Gate, the secrets of which
I neither know nor can tell.
No one but John could have done this,
For no one could even have seen   6370
A gate and a window were there;
He'd made them invisible to the eye,
Available to no one but him.
      When she saw the open gate
And the sun, which she had not seen   6375
In so long, shining through,
Her blood sang with joy
And she said there was nothing more
She could want; she was out of hiding,
She needed no new lodging.   6380
She walked into the orchard
And found it delightful. In the middle
Grew a beautifully grafted
Shrub, leafy and loaded
With flowers from top to bottom;   6385
Its branches had been trained to grow
Toward the ground, and nearly all
Hung low above the grass,
Except toward the top, where it opened
Out and grew straight toward the sun.   6390

Nothing could have suited her better,
For spreading beyond this grafted
Shrub was a wonderful meadow,
And the summer sun was never
So warm as now, at noon,   6395
Though its rays could not pierce the shrub.
It was John, of course, who had planned
Its tentlike shape and directed
Its growth. And there Fenice
Made herself a bed   6400
And happily spent the day.
The orchard was surrounded by a high
Wall, connected to the tower,
So no one could get in, unless
They entered through the tower.   6405
        Fenice was completely contented:
She relished everything around her,
The flowers, the leaves, the grass.
Nothing was missing. Her lover
Came, and she was free to embrace him.   6410
        In hunting season, when sparrow
Hawks and baying hounds
Would round up quail and partridge,
It happened that a Thracian knight,
Young, unmarried, lively,   6415
And honored for his courage and skill,
Was out hunting one day
And wandered close to the tower.
His name was Bertrand. His hunting
Hawk had flown away,   6420
After missing a fleeing lark,
And Bertrand was worried: losing

So good a hawk would be deeply
Unpleasant. He'd seen it land
On the tower, then drop to the orchard,   6425
Where it quietly alighted, which pleased
Bertrand, for now he could catch it.
As Cligès had done, once,
He managed to climb the wall—
And what he saw, on the other   6430
Side, were Cligès and Fenice,
Sleeping, naked. "My God!
What's this?" he wondered. "I'm seeing
A miracle. It's Cligès—yes, yes,
And is that the empress with him?   6435
Lord, she's so much like her
It can't be anyone else:
Her nose—her mouth—her forehead—
All exactly the same.
Nature never made   6440
Two women more alike.
Whatever I see in this lady
Is just what I've seen in the empress.
If she's really alive, I'd have
To swear she is the empress."   6445
Just then a ripened pear
Fell, and struck Fenice's
Ear, and she woke, and jumped,
And saw Bertrand, and screamed,
"My love, my love, we're dead!   6450
I see Bertrand! If he gets
Away, we're caught in a trap:
He'll say he's seen us: he will!"
Then Bertrand knew it truly

Was the empress he'd seen.   6455
And he knew he had to flee,
For Cligès had brought his sword,
When he came to the orchard; Bertrand
Could see it lying in front of
The bed. And Cligès snatched it   6460
Up, and came running, and Bertrand
Ran as fast as he could
And was almost over the wall,
Almost on the other side,
When Cligès came up behind him,   6465
And raising his sword high
Gave a furious swing and sliced off
Bertrand's leg, below
The knee, like an apple-tree branch.
But Bertrand got away,   6470
Badly wounded, and maimed.
And when his men, who were waiting,
Saw how he'd been treated
They were almost insane with anger,
Demanding to know who had done   6475
This ghastly thing to their lord.
"Not a word," he ordered, "just help me,
Get me up on my horse.
These are matters for the emperor's
Ear, and only the emperor.   6480
Don't worry: the man who's done
This thing had better be afraid
For his life, for he'll soon lose it."
        So they helped him up on his horse,
Saddened and shocked, and rode   6485
Sorrowfully back to the city.

It was more than twenty miles
Before they reached the court,
And seeing them come, everyone
Rushed out as fast as they could. 6490
And there, in public, in front of
The emperor, Bertrand declared
He'd just returned from a place
Where he'd seen the empress, alive
And completely naked, alone 6495
In an orchard, under a grafted
Shrub, with Cligès. They called him
A liar. Some said he was crazy.
The entire city boiled
With the news, which spread like fire. 6500
But others suggested, wisely,
That the emperor go to this tower
Himself. Followed by a wild,
Shouting mob, the emperor
Went, but no one was there, 6505
For Fenice and Cligès had left,
Led away to a safer
Place by Thessala, who assured them
That should they see, by any
Chance, people following 6510
After, hoping to catch them,
There was nothing they needed to fear,
For no one could possibly see them
Or come any closer to where
They were than a long crossbow 6515
Shot, fired from a tower.
The emperor stood in the tower
They'd left, and ordered John

Arrested, and held in chains,
Declaring he'd hang him, and burn him,   6520
And throw his ashes to the wind,
For the shame and dishonor he'd caused.
John would receive exactly
What John deserved, a worthless
Reward for sheltering the emperor's   6525
Nephew and his wife in the tower.
"It's true, by God," said John.
"I won't tell you lies,
And I won't hide a thing,
But nothing I did was wrong,   6530
For a man who's owned must obey
His lawful owner. I can't
Be blamed, for I couldn't refuse
Anything he told me to do.
It's the simple truth that he owns   6535
Me, as he owns this tower."
"No, John, the tower
Is yours." "Mine, my lord?
I myself am not mine,
Whatever I have is not mine   6540
Unless he lets me have it.
But if it's going to be said
My master has wronged you, my lord,
I'll stand right here and defend him,
Without waiting for his orders.   6545
What gives me the courage to say
Exactly what I think, exactly
What's in my heart, even
If it seems like total folly,
Is knowing I'm as good as dead.   6550

Let everything be as God wills!
And if I die for my master
That's not a dishonorable death.
The whole world knows,
My lord, what you swore to your brother,   6555
In a solemn, lawful oath:
Cligès was to be your heir
And succeed you as emperor. He's now
In exile; may God protect
And restore him! And you're responsible   6560
For breaking your promise never
To marry. Marry you did,
And so you wronged Cligès.
He did you no wrongs. And if
I'm put to death on his   6565
Account, if I die for him,
And unjustly, he'll revenge my death,
If he lives. Now do as you wish.
If I die, you'll die, too."
          So angry he broke in a furious   6570
Sweat, hearing these words
And knowing them true, the emperor
Said, "John, you shall live
Until your master's captured.
He's committed serious offenses   6575
Against me, though I loved him deeply,
And never thought of cheating him.
But you'll have to be held in prison.
If you know where your master's gone,
Tell me, I command you!" And John   6580
Answered, "Do you think I could do
Such a horrible thing? You'd have to

Tear the life from my body
Before I'd tell you where
To find him—even assuming   6585
I knew. And I don't, in the name
Of God: I've no more idea
Than you do, where he went.
But your jealousy, my lord, is a joke.
Your anger frightens me   6590
So little that I'm going to tell you,
Even if no one believes me,
Exactly how you've been swindled.
On your wedding night they gave you
A drink, and that's what did it,   6595
It cheated you out of your marriage.
Ever since then, you've only
Dreamed whatever happened
At night, the pleasure you took
With your wife: you were always asleep   6600
And dreaming, and you liked those dreams
And woke up thinking they'd really
Happened, you'd really held her
In your arms. But it never happened.
She'd already given her heart   6605
To Cligès; for him she pretended
To be dead; he trusted me
And told me; and he put her in my tower,
Which by law was really his.
You shouldn't be angry at me: 6610
I'd deserve to be hung or broiled
If I ever said no to my master
And refused to do what he wanted."
        Remembering the drink he'd so much

Enjoyed, by which Thessala   6615
Had bewitched him, Alis understood
For the very first time that he'd never
Been able to possess his wife
Except in dreams. He knew
It was true; every pleasurable   6620
Moment had been nothing but a lie.
And he swore he'd have revenge
For the cruel insult, and the shame,
Inflicted on him by the traitor
Who'd stolen away his wife,   6625
Or his life would be utterly empty.
"Hurry, quick!" he cried.
"As far away as Germany—
I don't want a castle, a town,
A city, left unsearched!   6630
Whoever captures these two
Will be dearer to me than anyone!
Go now, hunt them down,
However far they've gone!"
And they all hurried, as they had to,   6635
And hunted all day long.
But Cligès had many good friends
Who would rather hide him away,
If they could, than take him captive
And bring him back to court.   6640
For fifteen days they hunted
And hunted, and wore themselves down.
But Thessala led her mistress
And Cligès by such safe and certain
Arts and enchantments that they never   6645
Needed to fear the emperor's

Forces. They slept in no cities
Or towns, but enjoyed anything
They wanted, and more than before,
For Thessala knew their desires   6650
And brought them whatever they wished for.
And after fifteen days
Their pursuers gave up and went home.
But Cligès didn't rest on his laurels:
He went in search of King Arthur,   6655
His uncle, and though it took him
Time, he found him, and complained
Of his other uncle, the emperor,
Who'd tried to cheat him out of
The throne, though Alis had sworn   6660
To Cligès's father never
To marry, and remain childless—
A solemn pledge he'd faithlessly
Broken. And Arthur assured
His nephew he'd sail his navy   6665
Straight to Constantinople,
A thousand boats loaded
With knights, three thousand with soldiers—
So many men that no city
Or town or castle would be strong   6670
Enough to withstand their assault.
You may be certain that Cligès
Was careful not to forget
His thanks for this assistance!
The king immediately summoned   6675
All the high barons of his realm,
And had them find and equip
Ships, and galleys, and barges,

Heap them high with shields
And lances, with armor and whatever   6680
Knights required for warfare.
Arthur planned to set
In motion an army larger
Than Alexander's or Caesar's.
He called up men from England,   6685
Flanders, Normandy, Brittany,
France, and as far away
As the passes of Spain. He was ready
To send them out to sea,
But messengers came from Greece,   6690
Bearing news that kept
The king and his people from sailing.
The messengers brought John
Along, knowing his word
Would be trusted, for he'd never in all   6695
His life said anything untrue
Or carried a false message.
The messengers were Greek
Barons, searching for Cligès.
They were clearly overjoyed   6700
To have finally found him. And they said,
"May God preserve you, my lord,
In the name of all Greece,
Which is yours. You're now the lawful
Ruler of the empire, and lord   6705
Of Constantinople. You've yet
To hear the news, but your uncle
Died of pain and grief,
After his men could not find you.
His sorrow drove him mad.   6710

He would not eat or drink,
And died in a frenzied fit.
Good our lord, come home!
All your barons want you
Back, longing for you   6715
To return and be made our emperor."
There were those whom this news delighted,
But others would have much preferred
To leave their homes and have
Arthur's huge army set sail   6720
For fighting and plundering in Greece.
But the expedition was canceled;
Arthur discharged his army,
All of whom went home.
And Cligès quickly made ready   6725
To return to Greece, where he longed
To be; he refused to linger.
As soon as he could, he said
Farewell to the king and his friends,
Then took Fenice, and left,   6730
And headed straight for Greece,
Where the joyous welcome they gave him
Was fitting and proper for their lord.
Cligès and Fenice were married,
And both were crowned at once.   6735
He'd made his beloved his wife,
And called her "wife" and "beloved,"
And neither title hurt her,
For he loved her as one loves his beloved,
And she in turn loved him   6740
As a woman should love her lover.
Their love grew greater every

Day; he never betrayed
Their love, nor spoke harsh words.
Nor was she shut away,   6745
Like those who became empress
Later on, for later
Emperors were always afraid
Their wives were likely to deceive them,
All of them having heard,   6750
And remembering well, how Fenice
Had tricked Emperor Alis,
First with the potion he'd drunk,
And then in other ways.
Which is why, even today,   6755
In Constantinople the empress
Is always locked away,
No matter how noble she may be,
For their husbands never trust them,
Remembering what happened before.   6760
They're shut in a room, as if
In prison, for fear of the harm
They can do; it's not to shield them
From the sun! No uncastrated
Males are admitted, which stops   6765
Love from working its charms.
And here Chrétien stops.

Afterword

Joseph J. Duggan

In the Prologue to *Cligès,* Chrétien de Troyes identifies himself as the author of *Erec and Enide* but does not mention any of his other romances. *Cligès* is therefore likely the second in order of his five extant major works, the three others being *Yvain, Lancelot,* and *Perceval.* Under whose patronage Chrétien wrote *Cligès* may never be known. Features of *Erec and Enide* indicate that he composed this romance shortly after 1169 for a noble in the orbit of Henry II Plantagenet (1133–1189), king of England and suzerain of most of western France as far south as the Pyrenees. The Plantagenets were French-speaking descendants of the Norman conquerors of 1066. A noteworthy detail of *Cligès* in this connection is that when the hero visits England in search of King Arthur, he travels immediately to the castle of Wallingford and takes part in a tournament at Oxford, fighting on the Wallingford side. Wallingford was a center of power for the Empress Matilda, mother of Henry II, in her struggles against King Stephen of England, and in 1155, the year after he acceded to the throne, Henry held at Wallingford a council at which he had the barons swear fidelity to his sons, Willam and Henry. As in *Erec and Enide,* Chrétien mentions many other English placenames in

Cligès: Dover, Southampton, Shoreham, Canterbury, Winchester, the river Thames, and Windsor, all in plausible proximity to each other. Like Henry II, Arthur is said to have vassals in Normandy and western France as far as the passes of Spain. All this points to the possibility of a patron in the Plantagenet milieu, although patronage by a noble in Capetian France, possibly at the court of Champagne, can by no means be ruled out. A final note on the circumstances surrounding the composition of the poem: *Cligès* was likely presented to a patron in the expectation—emulating Alexander's generosity at Arthur's court (ll. 399–418) following his father's advice that largesse is the queen of virtues (ll. 191–216)—that Chrétien's efforts would be rewarded.

Also identified in the Prologue are several of Chrétien's lost poems, all translations from the Roman author Ovid, whose works were widely read in this period: the *Art of Love,* the *Remedies of Love* (l. 3), and, from book 6 of the *Metamorphoses,* two stories: the tale of Demeter eating Pelops's shoulder and the "Transformation of the Swallow, the Nightingale, and the Hoopoe Bird." This last is the tale of Procne, Philomela, and Tereus, and Chrétien's translation may be the one that is incorporated into an early fourteenth-century compilation in Old French known as the *Ovide moralisé* in which the tale is attributed to a certain Chrétien the Gois. *Gois* most likely means "inhabitant of Gouaix," a village near Provins in Champagne. But if Chrétien was from Gouaix, which is uncertain, he began as early as around 1170 to call himself Chrétien of Troyes, thus associating himself with that prosperous trading town, site of one of the four annual fairs of Champagne. Also at Troyes was the court of the literate Count Henry the Liberal of Champagne and his wife, Marie, daughter of Eleanor of Aquitaine and King Louis VII of France. Eleanor and Louis had divorced in 1152, and Eleanor, who held vast domains in southwestern France

in her own right, had that same year married the young Henry
Plantagenet who became king of England two years later. In
addition, Count Henry of Champagne's sister Adele was King
Louis's second wife. The court of Troyes thus had attachments
of kinship to the two major families that ruled large areas of
France, the Plantagenets and the Capetians.

Although we would certainly like to be able to read all of
Chrétien's translations from the Latin, the greatest loss from
among his early works appears to be his "Tale of King Mark
and Iseult" (ll. 5-6), most likely a romance or short tale about
Tristan and Iseult that is older than all other surviving romances
dedicated to these lovers except Thomas of England's *Tristan.*
The King Mark in question is Tristan's uncle, king of Cornwall
and husband of Iseult. The loss of Chrétien's text is all the more
deeply felt because the description of Cligès and Fenice's love
contains so many key references to the legend of the renowned
couple that it is rightly taken as a foil against which we may
interpret the tale of Cligès and Fenice. Lacking Chrétien's rendi-
tion of the legend, we must speculate what his reception of it in
Cligès means.

The principal French versions of the Tristan and Iseult legend
are the romances by Béroul and Thomas, both from the second
half of the twelfth century and each surviving only as fragments.
In addition, performed versions of the legend circulated in oral
tradition. Although he probably knew several of its variations,
Chrétien was certainly familiar with Thomas's *Romance of Tris-
tan* or a version close to it; like Thomas he plays on the words
l'amer "to love, loving," *la mer* "the sea," and *l'amer* "bitterness"
(ll. 543-54, 789-90). Fortunately, Godfried of Strasbourg draws
on Thomas's romance for his *Tristan,* which dates from the early
thirteenth century, and Béroul's version is close to that of Eil-
hart von Oberge's *Tristant,* composed circa 1170. Thomas was

also translated into Norse in 1226 for King Hákon Hákonarson of Norway as *The Saga of Tristram and Isönd,* which furnishes virtually the entire plot.

Thomas's *Tristan* recounts first the story of how the hero's father and mother, Rivalin and Blancheflor, fall in love and marry at the court of her brother, Mark; their counterparts in *Cligès* are Alexander and Sordamour. Like Tristan, Cligès wins from a powerful enemy the future bride of his uncle, who, like King Mark, intended to pass his kingdom on to his nephew but is persuaded by his vassals to marry. As in Tristan's case, Cligès falls in love with the bride. Like Iseult, Fenice is faced with a situation in which she must either reject the man she loves or share her body with both a lover and her husband, Alis. Iseult follows this second expedient, but Fenice, invoking the counter-example of Tristan and Iseult both to her governess, Thessala, and to Cligès (ll. 3118–3176, 5241–5246), refuses to do so, fearing the blame that would be visited on her should the adultery become public. But unlike the love of Iseult and Tristan, what Fenice and Cligès feel for each other is not caused by a magic potion, and Cligès might well echo the sentiments that Chrétien has the speaker of one of his two surviving lyric poems express:

Never did I drink the draught
By which Tristan was poisoned;
But my pure heart and good intentions
Make me love even more than he.
I should really give thanks for
Not having been compelled by anything
Except that I believed my eyes.*

*"D'Amors qui m'a tolu a moi," in Chrétien de Troyes, *Romans,* edited by Marie-Claire Zai (Paris: Livre de Poche, La Pochothèque, 1994), 1219–21.

Rather than simply carry out a clandestine love affair, Fenice arranges with her governess to appear to have died. Finally, like Tristan and Iseult, Cligès and Fenice are discovered living together in an idyllic hideaway, but unlike the fated lovers, their story ends happily in marriage.

In addition to its thematic influence, the legend of Tristan and Iseult inspired Chrétien to create engaging secondary characters of non-noble status, the builder and master of all arts John and the governess and sorceress Thessala. John in particular injects a unique note with his design of a tomb that no one can open except himself, his skillful construction of the house with secret passages that lacks nothing a lady might desire, even hot baths, and his defiant statement to Alis of his responsibilities to Cligès both as a slave and as a free man. The promise Alis made to Alexander not to marry is widely known, but only John has the courage to recall it to Alis's face, which causes the emperor such shame that, unable to avenge himself on Cligès, he dies a madman. In the interest they provide in the plot, John and Thessala increase the complexity of Chrétien's tale in the same way that such auxiliary figures as Iseult's servant Brangain, Mark's seneschal Dinas, and Tristan's teacher Governal do in the case of Thomas's *Tristan*.

The reader should note that Fenice's false death does not make her any less the wife of Emperor Alis, despite nonconsummation of the marriage: it simply reduces the possibility of detection in a society in which shame rather than guilt is the ultimate affective sanction for infractions against an accepted standard of conduct. The two tales differ radically in their moral sense: the love between Cligès and Fenice, who are attracted to each other of their own free will, can be justified by Alis's duplicity, whereas Tristan and Iseult's adultery, caused by the potion, must have been perceived as profoundly disturbing for the feudal order because it entailed violating the most sacred of obligations, the fidelity both of Tristan to his lord and uncle Mark and of Iseult to her husband, through no fault of Mark's. Whatever the nature of Chrétien's own poem about Iseult and Mark, he clearly considered himself a legitimate successor to writers of classical antiquity like Ovid. Lines 33–44 of *Cligès* are a classic statement of the motif of *translatio studii* found in the works of other medieval authors, the transference of learning from ancient Greece to Rome and then to France, where in Chrétien's view it now resides.

Chrétien claims in this context to have taken his tale from an ancient book in the library of the Church of Saint Peter in Beauvais, later the cathedral. Unless this is simply an appeal such as medieval authors sometimes make to a supposedly authoritative but nonexistent source, the ancient book must have been written in Latin. No trace of such a book has been found. Lucie Polak has discovered analogies between *Cligès* and the Persian story *Vis and Ramin:* Ramin is the brother of the king of Persia, who is rendered impotent by a talisman made by his bride Vis's nurse; Vis and Ramin fall in love; after a separation they are reunited and the king is killed in an uprising, leaving them free to marry. A story of this type is one candidate for the content of the mysterious book that Chrétien tells us he saw in Beauvais. Another would be the apocryphal tale of King Solomon's wife, discussed below.

The origin of the unusual name "Cligès" has been the subject of much speculation. According to a theory of Patrick Sims-Williams, it might derive from "Glywys," legendary founder of the kingdom of Glywysyng in South Wales, who became the hero of a lost "Lay of Glygis" and, in turn, of the late fourteenth-century Middle English *Sir Cleges* in which the eponymous figure is knighted by King Arthur's father. This hypothesis certainly seems more promising than a rival theory that "Cligès" derives from "Kilig Arslan," a ruler of the Seljuk Turks, and may well account for the name, but what might have induced Chrétien to situate major scenes of his romance in Constantinople, Regensburg, and Cologne?

The term "emperor of Germany" designates the Holy Roman Emperor. In Chrétien's time this was Frederick Barbarossa, emperor from 1152 to 1190, who held court, as does the anonymous emperor in *Cligès,* at both Regensburg and Cologne. It is in Cologne that in June 1171 he was negotiating the marriage of his son with Maria, daughter of the emperor of Constantinople Manuel Comnenus (1143–1180), who like Alis in the romance had raised himself to the imperial throne over an older brother's claims. To pursue the nuptial agreement, Barbarossa sent an ambassador to Constantinople with his powerful and ambitious vassal Henry the Lion, duke of Saxony and Bavaria, who was Barbarossa's cousin and the son-in-law of Henry II of England. When the negotiations failed, Barbarossa suspected Henry the Lion of having conspired with the eastern emperor. Barbarossa began to turn against his vassal when Henry the Lion failed to aid him at the Battle of Legnano in May 1176, and in 1180 he confiscated Henry's fiefs of Saxony and Bavaria. In the early to mid-1170s Chrétien would have known of the difficult relations between the emperor of Germany and the duke of Saxony, who was married to Mathilda, daughter of Eleanor of Aquitaine and thus Marie of Champagne's half-sister. Henry the Liberal of Champagne was Barbarossa's vassal for nine small fiefs but had been knighted in Constantinople by Manuel Comnenus.

The various elements of this contemporary situation reappear in *Cligès:* the imperial families of Constantinople and Germany, their marriageable offspring, the duke of Saxony. The sexes of

the candidates for marriage have been reversed. The court of
Troyes was favorable to the German emperor and thus hostile
to the duke of Saxony, and it is an unnamed duke of Saxony
who ambushes Cligès in Bavaria near the Danube. After being
unhorsed by Cligès, the duke halts his combat with the Greek
at a crucial moment, proving himself a coward. Such a shameful
representation of the duke of Saxony would not have been plau-
sible before the open break between Barbarossa and Henry the
Lion—that is, before 1176. On these grounds Anthime Fourrier
has ascribed *Cligès* to the period 1176–77, a date that has met
with general assent.

In its structure, *Cligès* is a genealogical diptych: a first panel
is devoted to the union of the hero's father and mother and
his birth, and the second panel recounts the love between
Cligès and Fenice and its consequences. Inspired by the *Tris-
tan* pattern, this form of organization became after Chrétien
a type, imitated by a number of thirteenth-century authors
of romance. Kinship was an element of prime importance in
medieval society, manifesting itself not just in the sphere of
aristocratic concern for the prestige of one's lineage but in the
most basic legal principles, under which a person could be held
responsible for the actions of relatives. In *Cligès,* the two suc-
cessive movements in the plot unite the ruling dynasties first
of Constantinople and Arthurian Britain, then of the two great
successors to the Roman Empire of antiquity, the Byzantine Em-
pire and the Holy Roman Empire. That Sordamour is Gawain's
sister and thus the niece of King Arthur is Chrétien's innova-
tion, contained in no other medieval source, including his other
romances and that most successful rewriting of history in the
Arthurian vein, Geoffrey of Monmouth's *History of the Kings of
Britain* (ca. 1136).

The process by which Alexander and Sordamour fall in love

highlights several themes of late twelfth-century literature that
derive ultimately from the troubadours who composed courtly
lyric poems in the language of southern France, Occitan. To
understand the refreshing novelty of what Chrétien is describ-
ing, it is important to realize that marriages between nobles
in this period were social and political alliances arranged by
young people's families. Love as the force behind a marriage
as momentous as that of Alexander and Sordamour was the
stuff of romance, and the romance as a genre was still of recent
invention in Chrétien's time. His principal model for depict-
ing spontaneous attractions between man and woman was the
Romance of Eneas (ca. 1155), an adaptation of Virgil's *Aeneid* in
which the characters are depicted as conforming in their physi-
cal and social aspects to the expectations of a twelfth-century
audience. The *Eneas* treats extensively the love between Eneas
and Lavinia, a topic barely mentioned by Virgil. Chrétien was
familiar also with the *Romance of Thebes* (see ll. 2520–24) and
with early versions of the *Romance of Alexander,* which provided
a source for the name "Alexander" and the scene in which he is
knighted.

A significant development in twelfth-century French society
that profoundly affected the genre of the romance was an inter-
est in the workings of the mind. Analysis of what a character
who was in love was thinking and feeling about the beloved
was achieved mainly through the internal monologue. Two such
monologues set out for the reader what Alexander (ll. 622–
869) and Sordamour (ll. 894–1044) are experiencing. They are
marked by changing emotions, description of the torments of
love, shifts into the interior dialogue mode, contemplation of the
nature of Love viewed as an allegorical figure, and the planning
of future actions. Speculation about love is couched in meta-
phors of a type that in this period has already been rendered

popular by the troubadours: Love wounds the young person
with its arrow; the eyes and the heart, once friends, have now
betrayed the lover; the beloved's eyes shine like burning candles;
the colors of her face are like roses and lilies, her teeth like
ivory; love is a pleasant sickness of which the beloved is at once
cause and cure. Alexander evokes a theory, based in ancient
Greek philosophy, of the physiological trajectory of love, pass-
ing into the heart through the eyes without affecting them but
causing the heart to burst into flame like the candle in a lantern
(ll. 713–715). All this ratiocination is accompanied by such symp-
toms as paleness, sighing, yawning (viewed in the Middle Ages
as a disturbance brought on by extreme agitation), sobbing,
and sleeplessness, mentioned either in Ovid's works or in the
Romance of Eneas. Extensive internal analysis is symptomatic of
a new age in which the interior life is recognized and examined,
and the romance is the genre that most intensely partakes of the
new mentality.

In this connection one should remember that Alexander is de-
scribed at the age at which young men of the high nobility were
knighted—that is, almost fifteen (as is Cligès: see l. 2745). We
can imagine Sordamour as probably younger still. In any case,
it is Arthur's queen who eventually brings the secret thoughts
of the young people to light and who gives Sordamour away to
Alexander in marriage.

The second panel of the diptych highlights the dangers of
adulterous passion, and it is not by chance that such a prospect
should be evoked in the context of an arranged marriage in
which neither party has shown any inclination for the other and
in which the bride-to-be is not even asked for her consent. Dis-
pensing with lengthy dissection, Chrétien has Cligès and Fenice
fall in love at first glance, before she even knows his name. This
time Thessala is the intermediary who recognizes the sweet sick-

ness of love when Fenice describes her symptoms. Fenice is
not shown engaging in internal analysis until Cligès has left for
England, after which she turns over in her mind the possible
meanings of what he has said to her before leaving and the im-
plications of her feelings toward him, crowning her thoughts
with a proverb (ll. 4558–4559), a common practice in medieval
romance. Thessala is a native of Medea's homeland, Thessaly,
and thus skilled at necromancy. The potion she concocts that
deludes Alis into thinking he has made love to his wife produces
the same effect as Iseult's substitution of the serving-woman
Brangain for herself in King Mark's bed on the wedding night —
namely, to protect a bride who loves someone other than her
husband. Here, however, the man Fenice loves serves the drink
to the husband.

The issue of consent as an ingredient in marriage is a possible
thematic concern of Chrétien. The secular model of marriage,
in which the union derives legitimacy from the consent of the
families of the betrothed, was in this period gradually giving way
to the ecclesiastical model, which involved not just the church's
blessing but the consent of both parties. By contrasting the woes
of Fenice and Cligès with the socially untroubled courtship
and marriage of Sordamour and Alexander, Chrétien may be
casting his vote for the practical advantages to society of the
consensual model.

The love Fenice willingly consents to is that of the nephew of
her betrothed, and only the ordeal of the false death saves her
from a life in which the alternatives would be either frustration
or adultery. Fenice herself proposes this stratagem, in keeping
with the meaning of her name, "Phoenix," the bird that lives
for five hundred years, dies in fire, and rises from its ashes to
live again, as was recorded in medieval bestiaries. Curiously,
however, Chrétien does not evoke the bird's death and rebirth,

citing only the beauty and uniqueness of the phoenix as associations appropriate to his heroine. That the artifice is of Fenice's design is significant, for she takes the initiative in resolving the dilemma of her existence in a more forceful and effective way than any other female character in Chrétien's romances.

The feigning of death to escape a husband whom the woman does not desire in favor of a lover who will carry her off is ascribed in a medieval apocryphal story, acknowledged by Chrétien in ll. 5857-58, to the biblical King Solomon's wife, who was said to have lain for four days without moving in order to be able to give herself with impunity to one of the king's vassals. The tale has an antifeminist ring to it, although Chrétien does not appear to be using it to that end. He elaborates on the legend by introducing the three doctors from the renowned medical school of Salerno who torture Fenice unsuccessfully until, in what might be seen as a comic development, they are thrown to their death by more than a thousand outraged women of the town.

But love is far from the sole thematic concern in *Cligès:* equal attention is given to the military exploits of the young Greek noblemen. Alexander proves his worth by fighting in defense of Arthur at Windsor Castle and taking the traitor Angrès prisoner just after the great king makes him and his twelve companions knights. The valor of Cligès, in contrast, emerges before he is knighted, in the general battle between his forces and those of the duke of Saxony's nameless nephew, whom he unhorses. A more serious test comes in his defense of the interests of Alis against the duke and his men on the banks of the Danube. During this battle Cligès kills the nephew and several other Saxons, rescues Fenice from her abduction, and humiliates the duke, who withdraws from single combat with him. Some of these scenes are quite brutal. Before his encounter with the duke,

Alis makes Cligès a knight, ceremonial confirmation of a level of prowess that is already recognized by his having been accepted as the Greek champion. Cligès's renown in the Arthurian ambiance comes only later at the tournament of Oxford in which, disguised in sets of armor of different colors, he captures three of Arthur's most accomplished knights, Sagremor, Lancelot, and Perceval, and fights the greatest of all, his uncle Gawain, to a standstill.

In the case of both Alexander and Cligès, the confirmation of chivalric worth is sought at Arthur's court, which Geoffrey of Monmouth had represented in his *History of the Kings of Britain* as the most advanced in courtesy, refinement, and military acumen. The Arthur of *Cligès* is not the political center of focus that he is in Chrétien's other four romances, but he does represent the principal source of prowess and other knightly virtues, leading Alexander and, at his urging, Cligès to wish to associate with him as a means of gaining prestige. Chrétien may also be incorporating elements of martial strategy in this work as a kind of guidebook to how to make war most effectively. In this regard Arthur's ferocity in having four prisoners that Alexander had presented to the queen drawn and quartered within sight of the besieged partisans of Angrès is shown to be unproductive, merely encouraging the rebels to resist for fear of a similar execution. Entering a castle disguised in the enemy's garb, as Alexander and his men do, is, on the other hand, a stratagem that might prove useful in siege warfare.

A third thematic concern after love and chivalric prowess is the politics of dynastic succession. In late antiquity the Roman Empire had fragmented into an eastern empire whose capital was Constantinople and a western empire centered on Rome. Both Alexander and Cligès, lawful heirs to the eastern empire, are affected by actions of Alis, who first assumes the imperial

throne after hearing the false news of his brother's shipwreck
and relinquishes power to Alexander only under an agreement
that allows him to keep the crown and title of emperor if he
promises not to wed — that is, if he gives up the possibility of an
heir who might succeed him. Alis's fault is in following the bad
advice of counselors who persuade him to marry the daughter
of the western emperor. Such an alliance would in ordinary cir-
cumstances have been considered politically advantageous. In
fact, it creates problems for Alis because his promise to Alexan-
der is public and as such makes him subject to societal sanctions
that Chrétien mentions several times and that are ultimately
announced to him, in a situation fraught with irony, by the
character who has the lowest social status, John the builder.
Although it plays no significant role in the plot, the threat of
Arthur's intervention with the army he has assembled raises
the specter of war between Constantinople and Arthur's realm,
which includes England, Flanders, and France. The two empires
that trace their descent back to Rome are in the end linked by a
marital alliance, but it is a more legitimate one than was first at-
tempted between Alis and Fenice, since the bridegroom, Cligès,
is the sole rightful heir to Constantinople.

The struggle of truth against deceit in the dynastic sphere
has its counterpart on the personal level in the play between
illusion and reality, including Alexander's alleged death at sea,
Cligès's battle exploits in both Germany and England while in
disguise, the potion that makes Alis think he has consummated
the marriage with his still-virgin wife, Fenice's false death, and
the murder of the doctors of Salerno, whose main fault is that
they have seen through Fenice's ruse.

Has Chrétien succeeded in composing an ethically accept-
able counterpart to the legend of Tristan and Iseult? It is true

that in the end Cligès does something that Tristan could never do, making of his lover a wife (l. 6736), but is their adultery to be condoned? If it is, how can one account on a moral plane for Cligès's maiming of the worthy knight Bertrand, whose only offense is that he comes upon the couple lying naked in their garden? Is black magic more acceptable in a Christian context when the person on whom it is used has failed to keep his oath? Why in the final lines does Chrétien make Fenice, whose agony and entombment take on an almost Christlike aura, the pretext for the distrust that all the subsequent emperors of Constantinople feel about their wives? Chrétien has written a counter-*Tristan* to meet the needs of his sophisticated courtly audience, but the message he wishes to convey in this highly entertaining and amusing romance remains enigmatic.

Recommended for Further Reading

Medieval Texts

Fedrick, Alan S., trans. *The Romance of Tristan and the Tale of Tristan's Madness*. Harmondsworth: Penguin Books, 1970. [Béroul's romance.]

Hatto, A. T., trans. *Gottfried von Strassburg, Tristan*. Translated entire for the first time with the surviving fragments of the *Tristan* of Thomas. Harmondsworth: Penguin Books, 1967.

Laskaya, Anne, and Eve Salisbury, eds. *The Middle English Breton Lays*. TEAMS Middle English Text Series. Kalamazoo: Western Michigan University, Medieval Institute Publications, 1995. [*Sir Cleges*, 367–408.]

Raffel, Burton, trans. Chrétien de Troyes, *Yvain: The Knight of the Lion*. With an Afterword by Joseph J. Duggan. New Haven and London: Yale University Press, 1987.

Raffel, Burton, trans. Chrétien de Troyes, *Erec and Enide*. With an Afterword by Joseph J. Duggan. New Haven and London: Yale University Press, 1997.

Schach, Paul, trans. *The Saga of Tristram and Isönd*. Lincoln: University of Nebraska Press, 1973.

Thomas, J. W., trans. *Eilhart von Oberge's Tristrant*. Lincoln: University of Nebraska Press, 1978.

Thorpe, Lewis, trans. Geoffrey of Monmouth. *The History of the Kings of Britain.* Harmondsworth: Penguin Books, 1966.

Yunck, John A., trans. *Eneas, a Twelfth-Century Romance.* Records of Civilization, Sources and Studies, 93. New York: Columbia University Press, 1974.

Critical Studies

Boase, Roger. *The Origin and Meaning of Courtly Love.* Manchester: Manchester University Press, 1977.

Broadhurst, Karen M. "Henry II of England and Eleanor of Aquitaine: Patrons of Literature in French?" *Speculum* 27 (1966), 53-84.

Duby, Georges. *The Knight, the Lady, and the Priest: The Making of Modern Marriage in Medieval France.* Translated by Barbara Bray. New York: Pantheon Books, 1983.

Frappier, Jean. *Chrétien de Troyes: The Man and His Work.* Translated by Raymond J. Cormier. Athens: Ohio University Press, 1982.

Freeman, Michelle A. *The Poetics of Translatio Studii and Conjointure: Chrétien de Troyes's Cligès.* French Forum Monographs, 12. Lexington, Ky.: French Forum, 1979.

Haidu, Peter. *Aesthetic Distance in Chrétien de Troyes: Irony and Comedy in Cligès and Perceval.* Geneva: Droz, 1968.

Kelly, Douglas. *Chrétien de Troyes: An Analytic Bibliography.* Research Bibliographies and Checklists, 17. London: Grant and Cutler, 1976.

Kelly, Douglas. *The Art of Medieval French Romance.* Madison: University of Wisconsin Press, 1992.

———. *Medieval French Romance.* Twayne's World Authors Series, 838. New York: Twayne, 1993.

Maddox, Donald. *The Arthurian Romances of Chrétien de Troyes: Once and Future Fictions.* Cambridge Studies in Medieval Literature, 12. Cambridge: Cambridge University Press, 1991.

Noble, Peter S. *Love and Marriage in Chrétien de Troyes.* Cardiff: University of Wales Press, 1982.

Polak, Lucie. "*Tristan* and *Vis and Ramin.*" *Romania* 93 (1972), 303-16.

————. *Chrétien de Troyes, Cligès.* Critical Guides to French Texts, 23. London: Grant and Cutler, 1982.

Sims-Williams, Patrick. "Some Functions of Origin Stories in Early Medieval Wales." In *History and Heroic Tale,* edited by Tore Nyberg et al., 97–131, esp. 103. Odense: Odense University Press, 1985.

Topsfield, L. T. *Chrétien de Troyes: A Study of the Arthurian Romances.* Cambridge: Cambridge University Press, 1981.